Uncovering
the Divine Within

a journey of self love

Kerri AE Kannan

INNERCIRCLE PUBLISHING

Uncovering the Divine Within
Copyright © 2007 Kerri AE Kannan

ISBN: 1-882918-06-1

Edition 1

Page Design by: Kerri Kannan
Cover Design by: Chad Lilly and Kerri Kannan
Cover Photo By: David Neff

Are You Aware?
www.innercirclepublishing.com

JANUARY 29, 2008

TO KIM —

MAY YOU LIVE AS IF EACH MOMENT WERE YOUR FIRST AND YOUR LAST.

~ For Rani and Gaia ~

WITH LOVE & GRATITUDE,

Kenji Kawano

Table of Contents

Acknowledgments

There are so many people to acknowledge for helping me with the creation of this book that to name all of them would be a book in itself. First I would like to thank my parents and siblings for being exactly who you are and for helping me to be exactly who I am. Thanks to Naresh Kannan for supporting me in finding my path and continuing to encourage me even though I have now chosen to walk it alone. Thanks to Bobby Christmas and Joe Shaw for helping me with editing services.

Thanks to Chad Lilly and InnerCircle Publishing for your vision and publishing this manuscript. Thanks to my "Yes! Family" and especially to Phil Beaumont for sticking by and helping me to find myself. Thanks to Jamie Mort for so perfectly reflecting me and growing with me. Thanks to all the people who submitted stories and inspirations that are used in this manuscript.

Thanks to Jon Snodgrass for your work and helping me with my first big "Aha!" Thanks to Robert Bruce and Peter Cooper for moral support and guidance through this process.

Thanks to Paul Hasselbeck for encouraging me to keep going and to get this book out.

Thanks to Maria Albrecht for helping me to simplify my writing. Thanks to Lucia Capodilupo and Sam Horn for your endorsements. Thanks to Jouni Ilola for showing me that I am love and always encouraging me to be 100% steadfastly true to myself.

Preface

This book is an attempt to harness the ineffable and place it into a perceptual spiritual understanding of the way things work. Because of the nature of writing a book like this, by the time you read it, the information will be stale to the author and a new level of understanding will replace the one written. I hope this manuscript will help you to gain greater clarity and awareness on your journey.

The greatest misconception in all of life is that we are separate individuals. In reality, there is one consciousness and consciousness is all there is. In the illusion of separation, everything you can see, smell, taste, touch, hear is experienced as something "other" than you. Every challenge arises out of a belief that there is something "other" than you and from this belief arise all conflicts, feelings, emotions and all experience in perceptual reality. We are consciousness and consciousness has no boundaries or borders. It has no set ideas or limitations, it has no religion, political leanings, no familial role to play, no gender, race or circumstance. Consciousness is all there is.

Beliefs are learned behaviors and ideas created by the ego to define how roles should be played according to the rules set forth by our cultures, religions, political affiliations, family units, race, gender, age and circumstances. Each belief system confines a conscious expression into a box and each belief system is a form of control. When we start to discard our learned beliefs, we begin to know ourselves as non-dualistic consciousness.

Introduction

Our thoughts manifest what we perceive to be our reality. As eternal beings, we can't actually be harmed, we can only perceive that we can be harmed which seems very real. When we change our thoughts, our experience reflects the change in perception.

The thought comes first and the experience follows. Think of it as if you were living in a dream state. Our dreams are all created in our minds, and we view our thoughts as if they were on a movie screen or as if we were living the dream. Upon awakening, we recognize the event as a dream. If someone says something spiteful or hurtful to you in a dream, it happens only because you have insecurity and you are acting out your fears in the dream. Dreams are tools to help us identify what we believe in our waking hours. When we wake up, however, we recognize that what we experienced was a dream, and most of the time, we forget about it and never even mention to the offending people that they said something that we interpreted in our dreams to be hurtful.

In our waking hours, we perceive things the way we want to see them. If we are confrontational and argumentative, that style of communication will be the bulk of our experience. If, on the other hand, we are peaceful and loving, the bulk of our experience will be peaceful and loving. We create each experience in our minds first and experience the effects of our creation later.

It is easy to see how people might like to think of themselves as powerless to improve their lives. If we can fool ourselves into believing that our weaknesses are not our responsibility or of our own making, we can convince ourselves that we are not responsible for our own lives. We can say "These things always happen to me," or find other ways to avoid taking responsibility for our lives. By displacing responsibility, we perpetuate a feeling of helplessness and a belief that we are a product of our environment. Our excuses are what keep us in cycles of unhappiness, longing, and powerlessness.

By disavowing responsibility for our lives, we believe our own excuses, and in doing so, we give away our power. We may want love, money, security, respect, happiness, you name it. The problem is, until we can change our minds about ourselves, we will not experience the thing we think will make us whole. Thoughts of lack perpetuate more thoughts of lack, and until we make the conscious decision to take charge of our own minds and act in accordance with our higher purpose, the cycle continues.

We choose our perceived deficiencies as the platform for our greatest strengths, and it is up to us to correct our self-perceptions so we can recognize our greatest gifts to humanity. For example, for many alcoholics, their greatest gift is that they have lived through the experience of alcoholism and co-dependency. Once a person has recovered from an addiction and healed their life, they can use their experience as the foundation for greater service to others. As long as we see ourselves as separate from others or disown parts of ourselves, we will remain stagnant and unproductive, and our greatest strengths will elude us.

We are all born to fulfill a role in helping humanity know its perfection. We do this by recognizing our own. There is nothing we can do to cause another to grow. To heal the world, we must be diligent with our own growth process. We help others through our example, there is nothing we can do to help another except to accept ourselves completely and live life fully.

When we are born, we are sheer expressions of perfection. We have no life experience to compare to ourselves and have every reason to believe we are perfect. Through our experiences, we are taught many lessons, some true and good, some false and best discarded. Unfortunately, as children, we do not have the life experience to discern which lessons are true and which are false, we just experience our lives in a non-judgmental fashion and understand most of what we're told as being true.

We are born into the circumstances and to the parents who will help us experience the events that will shape our thinking. Our birth selection does not always mean that we are born into the most seemingly loving, nurturing, and supportive of circumstances. On the contrary, we learn best through contrast, and through contrast we identify the lessons we have come here to learn.

If you are here to learn the workings of the human mind, perhaps the lessons you learn as a child will be that you are stupid and will amount to very little. Through the contrast, we see our foundations for our greatest strengths and our gifts to humanity. Through our experiences we understand the meaning of positive traits, or talents, and negative traits, or flaws. During the formative molding, our thinking becomes distorted, and we formulate our role in bringing harmony, peace, and love to human kind. We do this by perceiving ourselves as different and separate from others. Through thoughts of being different, special, or flawed, we chart our course to self-acceptance, love, and fulfillment.

We draw the experiences to us that validate any thoughts we believe as true. The people who have the most influence on our self-image or definition of self are those who we have contracted to help us identify the parts of ourselves we need to heal. The people I thought hurt me in the past were reflecting back to me what I already believed. People who supported me validated my positive thoughts. Because my negative experiences had a tremendous influence on me, I did not look at the experiences in a favorable light or as a tool to change my thinking. From experience, I have found that all experiences are positive ones and only my perceptions are flawed.

I have a large spiritual family who I communicate with on an almost daily basis. We are all members of an online forum and daily, we help each other with our spiritual processes. One woman who is part of my spiritual group has represented a very challenging relationship for me. For a long while, we had major personality clashes about every few weeks.

One day, while journaling, I asked myself what she

represented for me and why were we always at such odds. Upon introspection, I realized that she represented a host of fears I had that related to my own self-image. After I recognized what she represented to me, I was able to let her be herself without reacting to her style of communication. The shift happened within me, it had nothing to do with her.

Today, this woman who I had constant battle with for a year is one of my dearest friends. I had to completely accept all of myself before I could see that the one I had been battling was myself. Without the experience of having her in my life and going through what we experienced, neither one of us would be as aware of ourselves as we are today. What seemed like a negative experience turned into one of the greatest growth experiences of my life.

Healing my self-perception is the only way I can change the way I experience my interactions with others. When I chose to see myself as flawed and different from another, I saw the polar opposite the flaw expressed in the woman in the forum. The flaw that I perceived created fear in me that maybe I was less perfect than she. She showed up in my face and pointed out the limiting self-perceptions I had that needed to be addressed before I could experience greater love. When I realized she was showing me my own insecurities, I stopped resisting her which allowed her to relax and the relationship healed. The correction of my limiting thoughts allowed me to let go of the self-doubt she showed me. When I addressed my insecurities, it allowed me to embrace her and the challenge disappeared. The experience was a gift because it showed me fears and limitations I needed to address before I could experience self-love. We are all made of the same divinity, and therefore, whatever we see in another, we see in ourselves because there literally is no other. When I say we are infinite, I do not mean our bodies are infinite; on the contrary, our bodies exist within time and space. When I talk about "we", I mean our limitless minds, our spirits, our souls, the part of us that is inseparable from God and every bit of energy in the universe.

The physical world as we know it is the chosen medium for our minds to be challenged and to create masterpieces in our limited definition of reality. We all need some restrictions for us to unleash our full creative capacity. Without these restrictions, we have no medium in which to experience ourselves, no incentive to grow, and no challenges to overcome. The transcendence of our limitations is what allows us to create the masterpieces of our lives.

As a person living in a first-world country, it is very easy to feel that God is unjust by allowing others to be born into circumstances that we feel are inhumane. There is no God outside of us, God is in us all. We fail to recognize that every single person has chosen his or her own path to enlightenment and we cannot judge what lessons others have come here to learn based on our limited perception. Working within the confines of our limitations provides us the structure we need to harness and unleash our creativity.

I have a background in interior design. I have much more fun working within the limitations of an existing structure and transforming the space than building a structure from scratch. The joy in most vocations is to meet the challenges and create solutions in spite of the obstacles. The same is true for our physical, emotional, and mental limitations.

Anything we can dream, we can do. We might not have the capability of growing wings and flying like a bird, but we can use our limitless resources, our minds, to figure out how to build flying machines. The challenges of the physical world are precisely the restrictions we need to stimulate limitless creativity and have it flourish.

The same is true from a more personal standpoint. We must go through pain to fully recognize the reality of our own perfection. Our painful experiences are precisely the challenges we need to stimulate our minds and understand our greatest gifts. In the same way the physical world is our chosen medium to unleash our creativity, our painful experiences are the chosen restrictions we use to understand our greatest opportunities for growth.

I now embrace my painful childhood memories as the tools I need to recognize and fulfill my greatest contribution to humanity. Through the lessons I have learned, I understand that I am perfectly created to fulfill a higher purpose whereby I gain the most joy.

My desire for you is, by the time you are finished with this book, to recognize how your painful experiences are the tools you need to understand your greatest contribution to humanity. I also hope that, through a new understanding, you will allow yourself to forgive those you perceived as causing you the most pain. If you can release yourself from the burden and pain you carry from these experiences, you will set yourself free.

We all want to attain true happiness. I don't mean short-lived happiness that we experience now and then, defined as our happiest moment. I mean true, everlasting happiness or joy. The reason we all crave everlasting happiness is because love, joy, ecstasy, and happiness is what we are.

I have been fortunate enough to experience true ecstasy on two occasions. Both times, it was after I was able to release some long-held limitation I had been carrying around. The release allowed me to feel the freedom of my negative burdens being lifted from my soul. I accessed the greatest feeling of love and joy that I have ever felt, as if I were part of everyone and everything and that all of my experiences have happened for a very specific reason.

There are no accidents, and all the experiences I thought hurt me were tools for me to gain strength. I did not think I was strong intellectually, I knew it throughout every cell. I was filled with so much love that I would burst open and consume everyone and everything with my love. I achieved the loving state through forgiveness and released another person of being accountable for my pain. In releasing another for being the cause of my pain, I released myself.

Before having these experiences, I used to hear people talk about self-love and abundance in their lives, but I never truly felt it myself. I never knew how to love myself and tap into the universal energies. No workbook was available to help me change my mind about myself. I saw myself as inadequate and would tell myself I was great, but never quite believed it. A series of events helped me to change that false perception and I decided to put what I learned into a book for others to use as a guide.

By taking the steps outlined in this book, I have found I am more accepting of myself and feel more personal power. I have come to the realization that I am a perfect expression of divinity, and my perceived imperfections are self-inflicted wrongful ideas about myself. My ego is what tells me I am inadequate, and my ego is not an expression of my divine nature. My ego is a compilation my self-made limiting ideas and perceptions that are entirely false. My limitations are my illusions.

Through the words and exercises in this book, you will identify your illusions and learn tools that will help you fully love and accept yourself. You will gain great benefit by simply reading the text, but if you desire to enhance your experience, you will gain added benefit by answering the questions. Do not feel compelled to answer any or all of the questions. Use the book for your process, in a way that feels right for you. You can always go back later and complete the exercises if you choose. When you ask yourself the right questions, your subconscious mind will give you the answers. You need only trust yourself, and the right answers will flow from you. Your subconscious mind will guide you in your understanding.

After accepting yourself more fully, you will notice a shift in your life for the better. You will see that you have been wrong about yourself, and you will also see yourself for the unique person that you are. You will touch on, if not come to, the ecstatic revelation that you are indeed perfect because you are made of God. God can only be recognized through love and you must love yourself first in order to experience yourself as divine. Upon fully accepting yourself, all you could ever want will be yours. The abundance of the universe will be yours. Step fearlessly in the direction of your inspirations and spirit will guide you toward fulfillment and love. Trust yourself and your heart will guide you in Uncovering the Divine Within.

~ *My Story* ~

*"Some misfortunes we bring upon ourselves;
others are completely beyond our control. But no matter
what happens to us, we always have some control over
what we say about it."* - Suzy Szasz

Throughout my childhood and much of my early adult life, I allowed the judgments, observations, and perceptions of others to define who I thought I was. I didn't realize that I had a choice not to allow the criticisms of others to dictate who I was to become. I did not realize I was using my experiences to build a false sense of self based on the ideas I adopted from others. The guilt caused by accepting the judgments of others as who I was led to deep shame and a sense of wanting to disown parts of myself. The shame led me to conform to a definition of self that was seemingly more perfect but was not my authentic self. I was allowing myself to be defined by these "observations" and was conforming vicariously to the desires of people around me. I didn't realize that I didn't have to accept the observations as my truth or conform to the definitions that others chose for me. Like many people, I drew my conclusions about myself based on my experiences. I observed certain situations and made a judgment based on my observations. I allowed these observations to dictate who I thought I was, and with each judgment, criticism, and observation, I used the experience to validate who I thought I was or who I thought I was becoming.

In preschool one of my teachers told me that I was a good artist. I liked the thought, and from that point on always had a love of art because I thought I was a good artist. Had someone told me that my artwork was not very good, I can imagine that I would have disliked art from that point onward. My preschool experience led to many similar experiences throughout my childhood in which my artistic talent was validated. As a result, I eventually went on to obtain a Bachelor of Fine Arts degree from the Rochester Institute of Technology.

Similarly, I used to love to sing and dance, so my parents encouraged me to sing and enrolled me in dance classes. I was in love with Donny Osmond and watched "The Donny & Marie Show" and "Sonny and Cher" every week. I had always been told that I had a good singing voice, and I thought my dreams of being a singer were completely within reach. I was loaded with self-confidence and knew I was destined for greatness.

When I was six, my whole world turned upside down. My parents separated, and for the first time in my life I was not getting the attention I needed. My father decided to move into one of the spare rooms in the building that housed his restaurant, and after a while, my mother rented out our home, so my mother, sister, brother and I moved out. At first we moved in with my maternal grandfather, and although ours was not an ideal situation, we got plenty of attention because there were three adults in the house: my mother, my grandfather, and his wife. It was not necessarily the most comfortable situation, but he had a big house and plenty of room for everyone. While we were living with my grandfather, our home that my mother was renting out burned down. We remained with my grandfather for the summer; then my mother decided to move us out so we could attend the same elementary schools we had attended the year before.

My brother, sister, and I were suddenly living with my aunt and two cousins in their little three-bedroom trailer. My aunt was physically disabled, and after spending a period of time in a wheelchair, had graduated to a cane around the time we moved in with her. In addition to her disability, she was understandably overwhelmed when instead of two children in her little three-bedroom trailer, she suddenly had five. My aunt was not an affectionate person but she did what she could to provide us food in our bellies and a place to rest our heads. She had very little patience or time to give any of us the attention that we needed. Although my mother had custody and was supposedly living there too, entire weeks went by, during which I would not see my mother for even an hour, not even enough time for one hug.

My father had weekend visitation; however, he owned a restaurant, and weekends were the worst time for him to have visitation because he was so busy during that time. I needed validation, especially from my mother, that I was important and valued. I was not getting nearly the amount of attention I needed. I started internalizing feelings and blaming myself for the lack of love I was receiving. The message that I was sending myself was that because I was not receiving the love and attention I needed, I must be unlovable.

Finally, after several months of emotional deprivation, my father remarried. I remember him telling us that we were not going back to live with my aunt or my mother. We were finally in a secure and stable environment. Even though we were receiving love from my father and his new wife, I still carried into my adult life the emotional baggage of feeling unlovable.

One thing I never lacked were instances of people telling me that I was overweight. Around the time my parents first separated when I was six and then about the time my mother decided to rent out the house when I was around seven or eight, I had two experiences that made me want to disown my body. One day, my paternal grandmother decided to take me on a shopping trip to Paramus, New Jersey. On our way, she asked me what I was going to be when I grew up. I answered her with all the confidence in the world, "I'm going to be a singer." She paused and then said, "Oh, well, if you're going to be a singer, you'd better be skinny, because singers are skinny."

I had never heard this news before, and I tried to think of all the singers I knew. I thought of Tenille of Captain & Tenille, Marie Osmond, Cher, and even the women on the "Magic Garden" show that I watched every day after school. All of them seemed skinny. I did not know who Ella Fitzgerald was at the time, or I might have challenged her. Since I could not think of any singers who were overweight, though, I concluded that my grandmother was correct, singers are skinny.

Around the same time, I was in ballet class. I had been taking ballet for three or four years and had to go to a new ballet school, because my original one was in another school district, and I couldn't get there after school by bus. I had only been going to the new ballet school for about three weeks when our teacher had us do Russian splits for warm-ups. I could not get all the way down to the ground. My ballet teacher walked up to me and called me a "fat tub of lard" I was hurt and humiliated. I went home and told my mother who immediately yanked me from ballet; however, the damage had been done. I believed the ballet teacher's assessment to be correct and believed I was indeed a "fat tub of lard."

I moved in with my father and new stepmother during Christmas vacation. The change of address gave me the opportunity to meet Andy. Andy was the kid on the bus who gained his morning pleasure from torturing me in the most hideous, disgusting voice he could possibly muster saying, "FAAAAaaaAAT, FAAAAaaaAAT, FAAAAaaaAAT" the entire way to school. Andy was also my first real crush, which made his verbal battery all the more painful.

The experiences of receiving inadequate love from my parents planted the seed that not only was I fat, but also unlovable or unworthy of receiving love and admiration from anyone. I blamed my feelings of receiving inadequate love on my body and blamed my "fatness" for every disappointment. My feelings of low self-esteem were reflected in many aspects of my life including my grades. I was never an A student, but I usually got B's and C's on my report card. While I was living with my aunt, I received one B, four D's, and an F.

Because of the experiences with my grandmother telling

me I couldn't follow my dreams if I was not skinny, the ballet teacher calling me a "fat tub of lard," the seeming lack of love I received from my mother, and the object of my preadolescent desires calling me fat, I subconsciously determined that I was unworthy of being loved because I was fat.

I eventually graduated from high school, was accepted to my first-choice college, and graduated with a Bachelor of Fine Arts degree in Interior Design. Upon graduating from college, I got a job in the Cayman Islands as an interior designer and lived there for a year and a half. While there, I learned much more about myself and started building my spiritual foundation. My stepmother was very devoted to Jesus and because of her dedication, I was forced to be equally active. Later, I rejected Christianity because of my inability to make the choice as a kid. My chosen spiritual path led me to read many spiritual books, both fiction and nonfiction, including books on Kabbalah and Buddhism, plus the Celestine Prophecy and Many Lives, Many Masters. I met weekly with a group of friends to discuss the passages in the Tao Te Ching, started to learn about and explore some of my past lives, studied self-hypnosis, numerology, and palmistry.

Every day at sunset, I walked five miles along the beach to clear my mind and think. I explored my thoughts without the prejudices of my family and people who knew me from my past. I had a clean slate upon which to find out who I was and discover what I liked to do. After eighteen months, when I announced that I was going to go home on vacation, my boss told me to stay at home because a Caymanian who had been interning there wanted my job. In the Cayman Islands if a qualified native wants the job that an expatriate holds, the

Cayman native is entitled to the position and the expatriate must go home.

I was disappointed to have to leave and was going to try to fight it. I had finally gotten settled and made some interesting friends through the Cayman Drama Society. I was also asked to produce the next show. Upon further contemplation, I realized that I was not happy there, and the only saving grace was the people I had recently met.

Three months prior to my departure, a dear friend, whose family I had adopted as my extended family, left the island and moved to Delaware. When I looked around, I saw that most of the people I had come to know in the year and three months prior to my joining the drama society were leaving around the same time as I.

After I got back to the States, I moved back in with my parents and had a hard time finding a good job. In my parents' home (the home of my father and stepmother) I regressed to the role of the child, and after several months of not finding the right job, gave up and reverted to my old limited-thought patterns. I was substitute teaching and working in my father's restaurant most of the year, jumping from job to job to try to find something that would pay enough for me to get out on my own. It was too late: I had already resumed my old unworthy thought patterns, so of course, the universe helped me validate those thoughts by bringing me jobs that would not pay rent.

In March 1996, my parents took the family on a trip to Hawaii. While there, I came across a copy of A Course in Miracles. Ever since hearing Marianne Williamson talk about it on "Oprah," I had been thinking I would like to study it. In

Hawaii, while browsing in a tiny spiritual bookstore, I saw the A Course In Miracles on a shelf. That was the first time I had seen it, and I knew that if I purchased nothing else in Hawaii, I had to buy it. I read it, and by the time we left Hawaii, I knew that fear was the only thing holding me back from having a fulfilling life. I decided to follow my dreams and start my own business for spiritually seeking singles. Unfortunately, I was still relying on my parents for a place to live.

I threw myself into my new job as a social director at a glatt kosher hotel while also trying to get my new business off the ground. This was the second season I worked at a glatt kosher hotel and loved it. A glatt kosher hotel is one that follows strict Kashruth guidelines and is a sanctuary for Orthodox Jewish people who, because of their spiritual lifestyle, follow strict food-preparation guidelines. The kitchen is set up so that the dishes, cookware, and utensils used for dairy and meat do not come in contact with each other and several rabbis oversee the kitchen and food preparation.

I can't say that all of the rabbis liked me, but I had my share of friends with whom I could have deep meaningful discussions, people who were not too closed-minded to discuss Kabbalah with a twenty-five-year-old spiritual Christian-raised seeker of truth. One rabbi even told me that I, a blonde, blue-eyed goya (non-Jewish woman) should become a rabbi. It was perhaps the highest compliment he could have given me.

Not all of the rabbis I came across were comfortable in my presence; some felt threatened by me particularly because I had been a student of Kabbalah, teachings that are traditionally reserved for Jewish men over forty. Some tried to belittle me in front of the large crowds we drew through our lively discussions, but I was sure of my spiritual foundation, and all I needed was a few people to validate me here and there to keep me spiritually and intellectually stimulated and nourished. The stimulation was reciprocal because students of the Talmud, such as rabbis, often question everything as a method of understanding, learning, and growing.

Being a creature of great daring and slight naiveté, I thought I could get my spiritual-singles venture off of the ground before I would be kicked our of my parents' house permanently in the next few months. I named the venture SEARCH, which stood for Stimulating Encounters and Activities for Relationships, Communication, and Happiness. The name suited both my own spiritual search and my search for a mate. Although SEARCH was never given enough time to fly, I met some of the most amazing people I have ever met through that vehicle.

November first rolled around, and suddenly, my time had run out. I had been living with my parents for three years and they felt the push to kick me out. I spent November with a dear friend I met through SEARCH who let me stay in a room in her house for one month. In December, I started house-sitting for my former summer boss who was going to be in the city all winter and needed someone to watch his house. During that time, I reached rock bottom. I found a job in a trendy mall restaurant where I discovered that, despite having grown up in the restaurant business, I wasn't cut out to be a waitress. I was so desperate to have a job, any job, that I was commuting an hour and forty-five minutes to get to the restaurant and was making peanuts. I cried often and loudly and realized that there had to be something better for me.

My brother came home for Christmas 1996 and persuaded me to move out of New York. I had two choices: move to Minneapolis and be close to my brother, or move to North Carolina and be close to my sister. Although I had always been closest to my sister, I decided on Minneapolis for reasons that didn't make sense to me at the time; however, they proved to be correct. Something inside of me kept nagging that I had to move to Minnesota because my future husband was waiting there for me. I moved to Minnesota, and sure enough, the day after I got there, I met him.

During my first year in Minnesota, I was still jumping from job to job. I found a decent job in a furniture store as an in-house interior designer; however, the longer I stayed there, the more I realized it wasn't what I wanted. I didn't know what I wanted, though.

I was getting married in April 1998 and decided that when I left for my honeymoon, I was leaving my job for good. This time, I would find something more fulfilling.

We got back from our honeymoon, and I looked into myself again to see where I was going next. I didn't have to worry about money anymore because my husband was making three times my earnings and encouraged me to find my dream. I had previously given a donation to a nonprofit called the Wholeness Center, which put me on its mailing list. Its newsletter had a small advertisement for a volunteer events coordinator. I had done that type of work with SEARCH and with a small theater company, and I thought I would be perfectly suited for that type of work, so I volunteered. I attended a few board meetings, and after six months, was elected to the board. When the president of Wholeness Center decided to step down a few months later, I was elected by a unanimous vote to take the lead.

During this period, I intensified my search for what I was calling my "Life Purpose." I figured if I was being given the gift of being able to do anything I wanted to do with my life, I was going to find something I loved and would want to spend the rest of my life doing. Healing was an interest of mine, and a friend in Cayman had been a Reiki practitioner, which remained in the back of my mind as something I would like to do.

One day, my massage therapist said that she would be giving a first-level Reiki class the next month. She asked if I would be interested. I jumped at the chance. I knew I would be able to help people facilitate their own healing; however, I didn't realize that a new level of understanding and spiritual awareness would accompany each attunement.

During the same time that I joined Wholeness Center and had my first Reiki attunement, I was tirelessly trying to figure out my life purpose. I had been given the gift of the ability to quit my job and a be supported by a loving husband who encouraged me to find out who I was, so I took on the task of finding my life purpose very seriously. I read What Color is your Parachute and many other books that claim to assist in helping you find your "right career," but none of the tools I found were giving me what I was looking for.

I started on an Internet search for "Life Purpose" and eventually came across an article by a man named Jon Snodgrass, Ph.D., entitled "Your Special Function According to A Course in Miracles." I had been a student of A Course in

Miracles, so the article piqued my curiosity. As I read, a certain portion grabbed me. Here's an excerpt from that article: "Your Special Function is the polar opposite of what you believe to be the reality of your own guilt, sin and victimization... what is missing is your gift, your weakness is your strength, your special dysfunction is your Special Function." When I read the passage, I asked myself, "What's my special dysfunction? I'm fat. No, that's not it. I don't like myself. No, that's not it, either. I don't love myself.

I realized that I had to learn how to love myself and, through my example, show others how to love themselves. This was my life purpose. I found that once I recognized what I must do, an immediate recognition of spirit came over me. I no longer blamed the people in the past who I thought had hurt me. Instead, I joyously thanked them aloud while dancing and jumping around my living room as a whirlwind of emotions came over me. Without their harsh words and judgments, I would not have so profoundly recognized that I am perfect exactly as I am. Without the context in which to see what I already rejected about myself, I would not have recognized that it was actually I who did not love myself. I already thought that I was fat and came to my own conclusions about not being lovable through my experiences. These people merely offered the context in which to understand what I already thought I was lacking. I recognized that in accepting myself fully, I discovered the unlimited supply of love that I could now feel at all times. My objective in writing this book is to show you what needed correction in my own thinking so that you can compare your own life experience and perhaps correct any false perceptions you may have.

~ *Defining and Limiting Ourselves* ~

Thus says the Lord of Hosts: "Do not listen to the words of the prophets who prophesy you. They make you worthless; they speak a vision of their own heart, not from the mouth of the Lord. They continually say to those who despise Me, 'The Lord has said, You shall have peace'; And to everyone who walks according to the dictates of his own heart, they say, 'No evil shall come upon you." - Jeremiah 23:16-17

I always thought "beware of false prophets" meant not to go to fortunetellers and psychics. I never agreed with that interpretation, because I have had several psychic experiences and know many people who are fully devoted to God and have the gift of prophesy. When I was researching Scripture and other sources for this project, "beware of false prophets" kept entering my mind, so I finally looked it up. I was surprised and delighted to find those words that so eloquently sum up my feelings about letting myself be defined by the projections of others. My interpretation of the verse is: "Do not allow others to convince you that you are less than perfect, for they themselves do not recognize their own perfection and therefore cannot recognize it in others. Follow your heart and the dictates of your conscience, for that is your connection to God."

When we allow ourselves to be defined, we are limiting ourselves. We are choosing to accept the projections of others and incorporate them into our definitions of self. During my childhood, when I allowed others to define who I was, I was making a clear choice to believe their judgments were true. I could have just as easily rejected those projections but since I believed them to be true, I allowed myself to be limited by them. I assumed that because these people were adults, they knew the truth, and I therefore accepted their judgments and incorporated their evaluations into my definition of self.

If my grandmother said the reason I couldn't be a singer was that I couldn't sing, I would have rejected that evaluation, because I already had the reinforcement from my parents that I was a great singer. There was no question in my mind about my ability to sing. When she implied that I had an imperfect body, I couldn't argue with her, because I already had investment in that belief. She was merely validating my belief.

Here's an example of how positive and negative reinforcement work: Let's say that you are a race-car driver, and you have won many races over the past twenty years. For at least twenty years, you've had the reinforcement that you were a great driver. You've never been involved in an accident or had a traffic violation, and one day, while you pull out of a parking lot, your car gets rear-ended. The person who rear-ended you said that it was your fault and you are a lousy driver. Notwithstanding that legally, it is almost always the person doing the hitting who is deemed at fault, you would automatically reject that evaluation based upon your definition of self.

Imagine now that you were not a race car driver, but still had a love of speed. You've still never gotten into an accident; however, you've gotten many tickets over the years and have to pay very high insurance premiums because of your passion for speed. Again, your car is rear-ended in a parking lot and the person says you are a lousy driver. Because of your numerous tickets and your high insurance premiums, you might internalize that person's judgment and accept it as truth.

The reality is that, until rules or laws created societal values, morals, restrictions, and limitations, it wouldn't have mattered how fast you drove. The moment law was set in place, if you didn't find an outlet for your passion, you were doomed to non-adherence to the law. The same applies to social laws.

I had to take a class my senior year of college in which we had to read a book titled Egalia's Daughters, a Satire of the Sexes by Gerd Brantenberg. Brantenberg presented a society where the women had crew-cuts, wore suits, eschewed bras, and were the dominant force in society. They were seen more for the power they had at work than the way they looked. The men, on the other hand, were seen as attractive if they were fat, short, and wore cute curly beards with bows. The weaker the men seemed in stature, and the cuter their beards and hair, the more attractive they were to the women. It may sound strange to you; however, is it any more ridiculous than our male-dominant society? The culture described in the book was one that was a satire on the social and cultural norms as well as the gender roles we play.

We conform to what we think society expects from us, and in that conformity, we act according to the expectations of others rather than allowing our true natural expressions to be our guide. The more social, political, religious, familial, and cultural rules we feel we need to adhere to, the less we allow the truth of our being to dictate how we respond to any given situation. The point where the rules we adhere to intersects with our desire to be who we naturally are is where we will face our challenges.

The removal of imposed obstacles gives us the freedom of personal acceptance. When we shed the rules that bind us and no longer care what others think about us, we find personal freedom and release the boundaries that define us. The removal of limiting self-definitions is what frees us to be authentic and fully loving.

Many of us have no idea where to start looking to release our limitations and negative self-definitions. We know that there are certain things about ourselves that we don't like, and on the surface we can even rattle them off as if they were a grocery list. What we do not recognize is where and when we concluded that these specific characteristics were unacceptable. We are also often unaware that they are all linked to a central core or root that branches off and manifests as symptoms of the rejected or disowned personal characteristic. We are so preoccupied with condemning ourselves for our perceived imperfections as compared to others that we have forgotten why we started beating ourselves up in the first place.

It is against our conditioning to fully accept ourselves as whole and completely love ourselves as we are. Most of us reject ourselves mentally because of negative experiences in childhood where we learned to accept only some parts of ourselves and reject others. We take over condemning where our childhood experiences left off. Why do we continually judge ourselves and others for what we perceive as imperfections? Can we as aspects of God be imperfect? What is an imperfection? Is it some physical or emotional trait that in the eyes of God is unacceptable? Is it possible for God, who is love, to create anything less than perfect, or is it a method of self-destruction that keeps us from truly experiencing love?

When we condemn ourselves for what we perceive as imperfections, we are denying ourselves the true love of self. It is not possible to halfheartedly love ourselves; we either do or we do not. We are all facets of God, and because of that, we are all perfect. If the above statement were not true, God, who lives in all things, would not be perfect. God is love and therefore, once you find love of yourself, you will find God.

Searching for the roots of our wounds is not easy. We must mentally relive the most difficult times of our lives, the events that made us feel the most inadequate. These are the moments when we were freely expressing ourselves and felt a choking of our spirit, the moments when we fell victim to insane judgments and believed that they were true. These moments are the pinnacle points at which our feelings of self-love and acceptance were crushed because of our false perceptions of our own imperfections.

Once we are brave enough to revisit the past and identify the core of our self-rejection, we are well on our way to loving ourselves again and finding our own true nature. If we do not, we will repeat the same patterns that keep us from disallowing ourselves to experience true happiness, freedom, and love.

~ Exercises ~

Write down something you loved to do as a child. Do you still do it? If not, why not? Did you outgrow it or stop doing it for a reason? What do you love to do now? What is your passion? Do you have one?

Can you think of any talents, such as creativity or the ability to figure out how things work? Are you a nurturing person? Can you express yourself on a very deep level? Are you able to communicate with animals? Write anything that you brought into your adult life that makes you unique.

Name between three and ten qualities that you love about yourself. Can you think of any special things that you know or can do?

Name between three and ten things you don't like about yourself. Is there a common thread among all the things you don't like about yourself? If so, write that down.

Were you supported in your development? Name as many instances as you can where you felt totally supported as a child.

Take a look at the traits that you don't like about yourself, compare them to the traits that you like. By themselves, can you see anything negative about these seemingly negative characteristics? If a child whom you love told you that he or she had negative feelings about him or herself, what would you say to the child to help him or her see past the perceived imperfections? What would you say to yourself if you were that child? Write your response.

~ **When We Attack** ~

"If we have not peace within ourselves,
it is in vain to seek it from outward sources."

> *- La Rochefoucauld*

A modern myth is that if we exert our dominance over another through force, we are acting from a position of strength. That is a lie. The only time we are exhibiting true power is when we act from a position of love. Love is our real strength and is exhibited through compassion, charity, gratitude, tolerance, benevolence, forgiveness, and other, similar, emotions, and actions. Fear, the opposite of love, is exhibited through jealousy, intolerance, criticism, anger, rage, judgment, and other, similar, emotions and reactions. We act out of love, or we react out of fear.

If I view myself as strong, I might react to situations in a way that I think a strong person would. I might not necessarily act from a position of strength, though. If I see strength as demanding that another submit to my way of seeing things, I am acting from a position of weakness and fear. The fear might stem from an idea that if it is not done my way, it will not get done.

What is physical dominance, anyway? When we leave the physical realm, our bodies will erode, and what we have left is our consciousness, our spirit. The good we have left behind, the good deeds and the positive ways we have left our impression upon the world, is the part of us that reflects God.

When we attack someone, three things occur:
1. We deny love to ourselves through the guilt we harbor after an attack.
2. We maintain an emotional wall of separation between ourselves and that person, thereby denying love to the other person and ourselves.
3. That person must have triggered a feeling of weakness in us, and the attack is a tool the ego uses to reestablish superiority or power over that person.

If we do not perceive that someone is weakening us or showing us our weakness, we have no perceived justification to attack. We all become frustrated, but if we identify our triggers, we are less likely to be thrown off in anger. I have chosen to stay at home with my children while they are young. They are both preschool age, separated by sixteen months. I spend most of my day entertaining them, spending a great deal of time with them at the pool and the park, with books, and fixing and eating meals. I make an effort to take about an hour or two each day to check my e-mail and write. It's not very much time to get all the things done that I want to accomplish; however, I have chosen to be a stay-at-home mother and would not have it any other way.

Because I have chosen to stay at home with my kids, often, they rely a little too much on me to entertain them. If I am doing something I perceive to be important, for example, working on a presentation, they interrupt me repeatedly.

When writing a speech or an article, my oldest will usually ask me to do something for her to direct my attention toward her and away from my task. She might say, "Mommy, would you please read me this book?" At which point I say, "Sure sweetie, I will read you a book in just a minute. I just need to finish this paragraph." Three seconds later, she will say, "Mommy, I would like you to read me this book." I will respond by saying, slightly more sternly, "I know. I just need to finish this paragraph, and I will be with you in a moment." Three more seconds will go by and she'll say, "Mommy, I want you to read me this book now." At this point, I might use my loud, mommy voice and say, "I told you that I would read you the book when I finished this paragraph. The more you interrupt me, the longer it will take me to finish this paragraph, and the longer it will take until I get to your book. Take your book in the living room and I will be there in just a minute!"

As soon as I reprimand my daughter, in addition to alienating my child, I feel tremendously guilty for behaving badly toward her. I have subconsciously perceived her persistence as weakening my ability to accomplish my immediate goal of completing a paragraph, and therefore lashed out in an effort to establish power, control, and dominance over her.

The proper and loving response perhaps would have been

to respond the same way the first two times, but the last time, pick her up and put her on my lap. Responding differently would have given her the love and attention she was asking for at that moment, and I could have finished my paragraph in peace without harboring the lingering guilt of yelling at and possibly emotionally wounding my child.

By choosing to respond from a position of strength and love as in the second response, I am able to consciously create a positive outcome. Instead of allowing myself to take out my frustration and fear in the form of anger at my daughter, I am allowing myself to fulfill her immediate desire for my attention and allowing myself to finish my immediate task of writing my paragraph. By approaching it from a position of strength and love, I allow myself to forgo the guilt associated with using "force" to get what I want. I also can still view myself as a good mother. This situation is a classic win-win.

Criticism is also a very cleverly disguised form of attack. When we criticize another, we are really saying, "I am superior to you, and I am going to point out your flaw." If someone made that statement to you, you would consider it an attack. When someone reacts adversely to criticism, is it any wonder that they might feel hurt and might retaliate?

The only constructive criticism is when the person being criticized feels good about himself or herself and feels enlightened or bettered by your evaluation. All other criticism is destructive because it accomplishes only separation and emotional aloofness. There is no joining of the minds and no personal benefit from having "flaws" pointed out by another.

The two ways we can choose to act in any situation help us to understand how we view ourselves. One way we can see ourselves is from a standpoint of love, and the other is from a standpoint of fear. If we act from love, we approach the situation from a position of true strength and want to figure out a favorable outcome for all involved. We consciously choose to create a win-win situation. If we react from a position of fear, we feel the need to dominate a situation and dominate another to get our way. When acting from fear, we create what we feel is a "win-lose" situation, which is really a disguise for a lose-lose situation. The guilt we harbor after attempting to dominate another is what makes it a lose-lose situation. By attempting to hurt another, we also hurt ourselves.

Take "road rage" for example. Lets say that Lois and Cindy are both on the road. Lois is trying to merge onto the highway, and Cindy is in the right-hand lane. Cindy feels no reason to move over to let Lois in, yet Lois is traveling at the same speed as Cindy and is running out of lane. Lois doesn't understand why Cindy will not move over, because there is nobody else on the road. Lois decides that Cindy is not going to let her in, so she guns her accelerator and quickly moves into the lane where Cindy is traveling. Cindy then tailgates Lois, because she views Lois' action as an attack or an aggressive form of behavior. Lois then slams on her brakes because she feels Cindy is following too closely and is trying to cause an accident. Can you see the dynamic?

Each is judging the situation and feels that the other is attacking her, thereby pointing out perceived weakness in the other. In our society, the ultimate weakness that we perceive is death. If we feel someone is trying to kill us, we must also feel that they are trying to weaken us by killing us.

When I was a high school senior, we had one special

privilege called Senior Lane, which was a type of a study-hall room only for seniors and there was no teacher assigned to monitor us. The room had a couple of couches, a television, and a soda machine. Each day during my Senior Lane period, I had long discussions with my friend, George, and every day, I walked him to his next class, because I had lunch following Senior Lane period and didn't need to report to lunch at a specific time. I thoroughly enjoyed our discussions and George's companionship. Another friend, Tom, who was related to me through marriage also had Senior Lane at the same time. Tom and I joked that we were cousins and had a pretty friendly relationship.

One day, George got into a huge argument with Tom, which ended in a fist-fight. Because I was friendly with both of these people, I tried to distance myself from the confrontation. I didn't want to choose sides and could see that both young men had valid points.

Because I did not choose sides, George thought I was siding with Tom, and he must have told all his other friends that I was ganging up on him. The next day, all I heard about was how I was siding with Tom and ganging up on George. First, his friend, Ann, got a hold of me and threatened to beat me up. Then, a huge, tough girl who reminded me more of a bull dog than a person threatened to throw me through a window. These things happened all because I consciously chose not to choose sides.

I waited all morning to talk to George, and when he wasn't at Senior Lane that day, I got quite perturbed. I am a person who gets things off of my chest; I do not let them fester inside of me. These accusations were bothering me, particularly because I spent so much time talking to George and believed him to be a good friend.

After Senior Lane, I went to the classroom where I had walked George almost every day. I went in and told him that I did not appreciate his sending people after me and threatening to throw me through a window, particularly since I wasn't taking sides and was specifically trying to stay out of the argument between him and Tom. I said my piece and left the room. As I was walking down the hall, I heard my friend, Jackie, say, "Ooooh, Kerri, George just called you a transvestite!" At the time, I thought the insult was laughable. I did have a short haircut and was one of the few girls bold enough to have short hair, but my sexual orientation was never something I questioned.

Because I had a short haircut, George may have thought perhaps my sexual orientation was something that I was insecure about. Had he called me a fat whale, it might have had some sting because I had psychological investment in my weight but being called me a transvestite was something that could easily roll off my back.

Later, I found out that George became a hairdresser. There are stereotypes in our society about certain professions and the types of personalities that they attract. I am not saying I believe a person's profession indicates his or her sexual orientation. I am saying that I believe George's career choice may be an indicator of the issues he was grappling with in relation to his comment. Because there are stereotypes in our society about men in the beauty industry, I believe the issue of sexual orientation may have been something George had been struggling with his entire life.

If George had no personal investment in that particular trait, his "fighting words" would not have reflected issues related to sexual orientation. We notice in others only the things that hold value for us. If we invest energy in a trait, it is something that we believe has value. Whether we personally believe it is of great or little value is not important. If we focus energy on it, it holds some value to us.

Issues of sexual orientation were of value to George, which means that he spent time thinking about it. Whether he is same-sex oriented or opposite-sex oriented is not the issue. He deemed the topic important enough to try to use it as an attack on me. Our attack thoughts are always an indication of what the attacker holds as valuable, not what the person being attacked holds as valuable.

I found the same to be true in the incidents that stand out in my early childhood. My grandmother died of complications from diabetes. She had been heavy most of her life and had unresolved issues with her weight. The dance industry is notorious for telling girls and young women that their bodies are inadequate, so my ballet teacher most likely had her issues about her own body; I was just reflecting back to her something that she disliked about herself.

Interestingly, one day when Andy was screaming "Fat" at me, an older kid who usually drove to school stopped him and said, "Andy, why are you doing this to this girl? You're fat yourself, so why are you doing this to her?" It never occurred to me before that Andy might be perceived as fat, but someone did. Andy identified his perceived flaw in me, and his daily torment was his way of trying to dissociate that specific trait from himself by targeting it in me.

When my tormentors attacked me, they each saw in me something that reminded them of a "weakness" they perceived they had. I triggered the response by just being me, and their attacks were really an attack on themselves. By trying to dissociate from a particular trait, they noticed the same trait in me. Had my "flaw" meant nothing to them, they would not have noticed it in me. Because they were subconsciously self-condemning for having the same flaw, they felt justified in their attack.

Attack is merely a tool the ego uses to try to elevate one's own feelings of self-worth by pointing out the same rejected trait in another. By paying attention to our attack thoughts, we will have a better understanding of what we view as important or lacking in our own lives.

~ Exercises ~

Think of the last time you felt anger, rage, jealousy, insecurity, frustration, or the need to criticize or judge. Can you identify the source of weakness you were expressing through your emotions?

Considering that we all react based on past experiences, what triggered your reaction, and what experiences did you base your fearful reaction on? If you can remember, when did you start to believe that concept was something to fear?

How did you feel after projecting your fear in that situation? Did you feel empowered, righteous, guilty, happy, loving, exalted, sad, angry or fearful? Describe in as much detail as possible what triggered the fear in the situation.

How could you have handled that situation in a more loving manner?

~ Choosing Our Experience and Families ~

"Every person, all the events of your life are there because you have drawn them there. What you choose to do with them is up to you." - Richard Bach

We are all expressions of life. Science can explain many things, but it cannot explain why we think and feel or what causes life and death. That inexplicable, untouchable part of us is our divine nature. We all share a common bond, a linking of minds, that we cannot undo, no matter how hard we try to maintain separateness from each other. Any time we feel uncomfortable about a circumstance, person, or situation, we are experiencing the product of our limiting egos. The ego maintains separation through our fear-based thoughts. When we recognize our true selves, our divine selves, we no longer want the ego to dominate our lives. We see that in our egoistic desire to control everything, we are stifled in our growth, power, love, and happiness. When we stop giving in to our ego whims and have them take a back seat to love, we start seeing love reflected in more of our interactions. When we start living from a position of love and acceptance, we notice love reflected in the way we perceive our world.

The love we are seeking is our own self-love. Love has nothing to do with how others perceive us. When we accept ourselves and stop trying to conform to the way we think others would like us to be, we tell ourselves that we love and accept who we are. When we accept who we are, we release the expectation that others will be who we want them to be. We release expectation because what we wish others to be is a reflection of what we seek to recognize in ourselves.

One of the traits that I was encouraged to suppress as a child was my sensitivity and seeming vulnerability to the opinions of others. Things affected me very deeply and still do, I have always had a hard time letting the criticisms of others roll off my back. Now that I am an adult, I find that the same trait that I viewed in childhood as a character weakness is now one of my greatest attributes.

Sensitivity allows me to recognize very clearly when something is bothering me, so that I can understand what I need to address in my thinking and can correct it. The most important things to me are my family and my personal development. I have found that the more sludge I can bring to the surface and release for the entire world to see, the greater my capacity to grow.

By delving into the depths of my own experience and bringing things into the light, I help others see their own vulnerabilities from a more human, loving perspective. It is not important that others share their experiences with me, but that my ability to tell others of my experiences helps them identify and heal their own minds. I now view my vulnerability and emotional honesty as among my greatest strengths, because they help me connect with people and allows them to see that we all go through painful periods.

Many of us do not see our childhood as perfect. Many people were neglected or abused, felt unloved or unappreciated. Children bury their feelings when they are not treated with respect, honesty, and consideration. Many children blame themselves if their parents' marriage breaks up or if there are financial difficulties. Children may carry the guilt of a parent leaving, or feel responsible if they are shuffled from foster home to foster home, because they may feel that they have done something wrong. They might feel they have done something to make their parents stop loving them, or they may identify some other aspect of themselves to blame for not receiving the love they need.

Children do not understand that adults have pains and problems. They trust that adults know all. They trust that as caretakers, adults are acting in the most loving way they can. Children do not realize that they are not lesser human beings just because they may find themselves in unfavorable conditions. Kids internalize feelings of guilt and blame themselves for circumstances that are beyond their control.

Because of circumstances, many children harbor feelings of worthlessness, an inability to be loved and give love. They feel they were abandoned because they were bad or unworthy. Too often, these feelings are brought into adulthood and manifest as adult behavior. If, as a child, a person felt that he or she was lacking something, unless the perception is corrected, it will manifest in the adult as feelings of lack and worthlessness. We may experience lack in many forms of negative thinking, and it will manifest itself in many ways, through an inability to experience true happiness.

If we do not feel at peace and fulfilled as adults, it is most likely because we have some deep-seated issues of self-worth that we must address before we can find what we believe is missing in our lives. As adults, we can plainly see how some of us treat others unfairly. We do not normally identify that people are products of their upbringing and have their own wounds to overcome. We expect adults, particularly parents, to know how to be the most supportive, loving people on the face of the planet. We do not recognize that most people have layer upon layer of issues to resolve before they can be fully supportive parents.

Unfortunately, the effects of "bad parenting" do not end with childhood. The effects manifest in the adulthood of the ill-treated child, and many times the behavior cycle will be repeated in the next generation, unless the people affected by "bad parenting" have the strength to look inside to see why they treat themselves poorly. The parents must dig deeply to see the root cause of their own pain that causes them to inflict pain on others. Once they find it, they must heal it. If the pattern is not recognized, it will be repeated. Unless the adults are ready and willing to face the pain of the past, they will not mature and transcend the thinking that keeps the patterns in place. They will, instead, deal with the problem later, on a superficial basis, or hope it will just go away.

Unless patterns are addressed, they do not go away. Denial that a problem or issue exists only creates internal conflict.

Until we address our dissociated thoughts, we create turmoil and conflict in our lives. Once identified and addressed, the conflict disappears.

Conventional wisdom tells us that no child would volunteer to be born into an abusive or neglectful situation. I disagree. We cannot know what the contracts are between parents and their children, so we cannot understand why a child may have chosen to be born to parents who seem abusive or neglectful.

The child and parent are not aware of why they have chosen to come together in this lifetime and don't know what has brought them together, so how can someone outside of that relationship judge the situation? I am not saying people should keep quiet and not intervene when they feel someone is being abused, neglected, or in need of help. On the contrary, we must all listen to our hearts and if our internal guidance tells us to take action, we must. All these factors play a part in the intricate karmic dance that we call life. The following story is an illustration.

Hannah and Rena were best friends in elementary school. Both were labeled as having learning disabilities, and each of them overcame her limitations by being true to herself. Both persevered when others told them they would not succeed. Both Hannah and Rena had to claim themselves in order to recognize their greatest strengths despite the judgments, criticisms, and opinions of others.

Hannah had always been the caretaker of her family. Her mother was a disabled diabetic who was housebound and incapable of taking care of herself, so Hannah's brother always relied on Hannah for everything. She played the role of the nurse and caretaker for her mother as well as a surrogate mother for her brother. Hannah had grown up being self-sufficient and resourceful when times were tough. She learned how to handle many tasks and responsibilities at a very young age. Although taking care of her disabled mother and younger brother was a challenge, she developed the emotional fortitude to overcome her challenges and learned how to deal with any crisis thrown her way.

Hannah wanted to be a teacher. When she was ready for college, she had a meeting with her guidance counselor to determine which college would be best for her. Because of Hannah's dyslexia, her grades were not commensurate with her intelligence, and the counselor told Hannah that she was not college material; she would be better off considering cosmetology school or some other route. That was not in line with her personal goals and ambitions.

Hannah abandoned the advice of the guidance counselor and entered a respectable undergraduate program. She graduated with honors and was accepted into a master's program at New York University. Coincidentally, Hannah ended up student teaching in the same school where she had gone to high school. On her first day of student teaching, she walked into the guidance counselor's office and told her, "I am now in graduate school at NYU, no thanks to you." She then stormed out and went to work with the kids.

Hannah found that teaching was too structured for her. She has since abandoned teaching for a more challenging and lucrative career as a building manager for one of the largest apartment-management groups in the Washington, D.C., area. She manages not one but several high-rise buildings and is perfectly comfortable handling the daily crises that fill her plate. The order and structure of the classroom, seemingly chaotic to many, was not the perfect fit for Hannah; she is much more comfortable dealing with the daily operations, requests, and emergencies of the hundreds of residents and employees who are now her responsibility in the residential buildings where she works.

Hannah's childhood taught her how to take care of people's problems and deal with them in an orderly, self-reliant way. She has also fully claimed her intelligence despite her struggles as a kid and despite her guidance counselor's negativity. She has risen above her childhood labeling and proven to herself that she is capable of things she might never have dreamed of as a child. By listening to her own heart, she has become very successful because she did not let anyone else keep her down. Her childhood provided her the foundation to take care of any crisis, and because she was also equipped with the tools of self-reliance as a child, she always held the belief that she was capable of achieving anything.

Like Hannah, Rena was labeled an overactive child. She came from an affluent family and attended private schools during her elementary school years. She was a very spirited and creative child, and her teachers had a hard time dealing with her "disruptive behavior." Eventually, at age sixteen, after being expelled from no less than six schools, she wanted to quit school and get her GED. Her parents agreed. Because of her experience as a child who did not have her needs met by the educational institutions, she grew up knowing what it was like to have special needs and not have them met.

Rena eventually obtained her GED and went to college. Today she has her master's degree in Special Education and is considered an excellent teacher. Her experiences as a child were her gift. She could see a need that had not been filled for her when she was a child, and because of living through the experiences she did, is now a positive example and an inspiration for many kids in the Special Education program in her school district.

Acutely aware of the need she fills, Rena takes her job very seriously. Had she not had such a hard time in school, she would not have so fully understood the serious need to provide the best education for kids with special needs. She approaches her work with love and integrity and is proof that one need not conform to the expectations of others in order to become successful. Her experience of feeling different from everyone else is her greatest asset and the foundation for her greatest gift to humanity.

Like Hannah and Rena, we are born into the circumstances and to the parents who will help us experience events that shape our thinking and facilitate our growth. Through these experiences we understand our positive traits or talents and negative traits or flaws. It is through formative molding that our thinking becomes distorted. When we choose to see ourselves as flawed, it is the healing of our self-perception that will allow us to recognize our special contribution to humanity, or our life purpose. The healing of flawed beliefs is what will lift the veil that obscures our vision and allow us to experience ourselves as complete and whole.

When we see ourselves as complete and whole, we recognize our true spirit and know the reason for our existence. Once we remove the barriers to knowing ourselves as complete and whole, the obstacles to understanding our life purpose are removed and our highest contribution to humanity becomes obvious.

In the following exercises, you will uncover the areas of your childhood where you expressed your spirit through laughter and fun. You will see where you were supported and where you were not. You will see where you were stunted and where you were encouraged in your growth. You will touch on your perceived positive and negative qualities and how you came to recognize them as positive and negative.

~ Exercises ~

Can you think of any unpleasant experiences or unfortunate incidents that happened in your childhood or adult life? How did each event affect you? How did you cope with your feelings? Search your feelings. Do you still feel emotionally scarred?

Do you feel responsible for this occurrence? Do you have any regrets regarding this event? Do you harbor any judgments regarding the experience? If so, write the events in as much detail as you can. Write your feelings toward all involved with this or these events.

Can you see any patterns among these judgments and the way you see yourself today? Do you feel unappreciated, stupid, restricted, fat, lazy, crazy, or do you have other feelings that you are not a perfect, lovable, worthy being?

Can you find a link between thoughts and feelings in childhood when you were hurt and your thoughts about yourself today? If so, how do these feelings affect your adult life?

Can you see a pattern or patterns connecting your impressions as a child and your thoughts and actions as an adult?

Can you see how these thoughts are ingrained in you after years of self-rejection? Do you see how your thoughts manifest in your body, love life, paycheck, or health?

~ **Contracts** ~

*"When the first Superman movie came out I was
frequently asked, 'What is a hero?' My answer was that
a hero is someone who commits a courageous action
without considering the consequences. Now my definition
is completely different. I think a hero is an ordinary
individual who finds strength to persevere and endure in
spite of overwhelming obstacles."* - Christopher Reeve

I believe in reincarnation. I also believe that we very carefully create blueprints or contracts for each lifetime. Within these contracts, we create a detailed plan of all the interactions and events in our lives. We have come here to learn, and the world with our physical limitations is the school we have chosen to be our medium whereby we learn our lessons.

Each time we meet or interact with someone, we take away the experience of the interaction. We cannot always point out what the purpose may have been for the interaction, but each person we meet affects us at some level. They might reinforce something in our thinking, help us to look at things in a different way, or maybe just remind us of someone we love. All of our interactions are significant because they help us to see what is working in our lives or perhaps what is not working. Each experience is an opportunity to reevaluate ourselves and to choose who we wish to be in that experience. We are always recreating ourselves anew and constantly evolving.

Our contracts with others help us grow. Our major contracts are with the people who have had the most significant influence on our lives. Whether we know the names of the people or not is irrelevant. These significant relationships can be judged as good or bad, but they are always opportunities for us to see what works for us or what might be an area where we can improve our lives.

When we feel most challenged, we are standing at the crossroads where our spirit wishes to go and where we think we should go. Our attachments to our beliefs about who we should be, who we are, and how we should behave are what create the greatest impediment to our spiritual growth. We feel that we should act in a specific manner or think a certain way in order to be accepted. We formulate these beliefs through our formative interactions and experiences and choose to define ourselves through the social, religious, cultural, educational, political, familial, and philosophical criteria. Our challenges are the exact prescription we need to identify and shed the limiting beliefs that keep us from expanding our awareness of our interconnectedness with everything.

My friend, Jan, shared with me a story that describes one of her experiences of living through a contract and seeing the interconnectedness of everything. Here is the story in her words:

One time, after I went through a trauma that felt like my spirit was broken, I put my entire life savings into a business. I chose an unethical partner, and within two months he took my business away from me. I got to the point where all I could do was watch the squirrels out the window. I didn't turn on the television, I went to the grocery store in my pajamas to get cat food. I stopped eating and withered away to ninety-seven pounds. I didn't know what to do so I did nothing. I got an eviction notice and finally one of my friends from my home state called me and I told her my troubles. She said, "Go get some boxes and start putting your things in them. I will come get you and bring you home." My friend didn't even have a car. She came to get me and brought two friends, one of whom I had never met. They all helped move me back to my hometown.

My friends dropped me off at my ex-husband's house and told him to help me and he did. He fed me and lent me enough money to get an apartment and to build another business in the back of his business. One of the hardest things I have ever done was to get up off the couch in my new apartment, with all my stuff in a big pile in the middle of the floor, and go build another shop. But I did and my spirit healed.

For six years, I worked on forgiving the one who took my other shop away, but I still had a little bit of anger.

My ex-husband and I developed a very close relationship. After six year's time, he died. I suddenly realized that if the guy hadn't taken away my other shop so quickly, I would have missed some of the last time I had to spend with my ex-husband. As a result, I was able to send him love and thanks from my heart. The friend who came and rescued me said she got a message from the universe after I got back saying it was sorry the ordeal was so hard on me but it had to get me back here where I was safe.

The whole experience taught me that God has a much bigger plan than I can fathom, so have faith of at least the size of a mustard seed and everything will be perfect. I now can see how every moment of my life has been valuable and has made me who I am today. I am also able to draw on these experiences and depth for what some are going through so I can help them. I am grateful to be here now. Here is the magic, God is the magic.

Jan became attached to her idea of what should happen with her business, which blinded her to the greater plan. When her plans didn't work out the way she expected, she became weak and depressed. When she was finally forced to her knees, the universe rushed in and helped her to see things differently. The moment she surrendered her plan to the universe, she was brushed off and set back on her feet in a much more supportive and fulfilling circumstance.

Whenever there is even a small willingness to see things differently, the universe rushes in to help us change our perspective. I once prepared a speech titled "Trash that Borrowed Cloak." In the speech, I told people that when we are young, we allow others to define us by borrowing their ideas of who we are. I called these ideas threads that we could either reject as false and discard or accept as truth and carefully incorporate that idea or "thread" into an intricate cloak that we use as a substitute for who we think we are. We call that cloak our "definition of self." I used my favorite examples of my grandmother, the ballet teacher, and Andy.

All these people gave me an idea or thread, which I could incorporate into my cloak of self-doubt and condemnation or discard as false. I chose to incorporate those threads into my cloak, thereby hiding or cloaking my true self. I described how all the people who influenced me had their own self-image issues and saw their perceived flaw in me. The speech was very emotional for me, and as I choked back the tears, I felt some kind of release.

The next night, I had a dream that I was giving the same speech to a group around a large round table. Andy was sitting to my right, and as I described the way he said "FAAAaaat" to me, he began to fidget and show signs of being uncomfortable. While I was speaking, I tried to console him by rubbing his back and leg, an effort to reassure him that it was all okay. After the speech, I gave him the warmest, most healing hug I have ever experienced. I told him that if he had not done such a great job of making me feel terrible, it would not have had such a great impact on my ability to reverse that feeling and heal my self-image. I told him that his being "mean" to me was the greatest gift anyone could have given me. The fact that I had a crush on him at the time only compounded my feeling of inadequacy and the affect on my ability to heal my thoughts.

After the dream, I awoke and a euphoric feeling of love, gratitude, and forgiveness engulfed me. I felt such an all-consuming love for Andy that I felt that my heart would burst open from all of the joy. To say that I forgave Andy is inadequate. I thanked him for being so good at pointing out my own cruel, harsh judgment of myself.

After the speech and the dream, I sent Andy a letter and

a copy of an article I had published a few years earlier. I told him, whatever he might think he did to me, to please never feel guilty about it, because it was something I had to go through in my personal development. I wanted him to know that sending the letter was part of my healing process, and if I was ever delivering a presentation in his town or area, I would love for him to attend and allow me to give him the hug of gratitude he so rightly deserved.

Upon reflecting on the experience, I realized that Andy and I had a contract. I chose him to deliver a message to me, and chose to have a crush on him, because the circumstance would increase the intensity of the lesson. Also, I realized that on a spiritual level, he loves me a great deal and tackled his assignment with so much fervor and determination that he wanted to make sure I learned the lesson well. It was through his love that he succeeded in pointing out to me the part of myself that I had already rejected. Every time he called me "fat" he was saying to me, "Kerri, this is the part of your mind that you need to heal to know your true self."

Think of the most difficult challenge you have ever faced and overcome. Chances are that after the challenge was over, you were a changed person. Overcoming obstructions to knowing our true nature is what the lessons on earth are all about. As I have said before, we learn best through struggle and deprivation, and because we are inherently infinite, we can handle anything that comes our way. There is a saying, "God doesn't give us more than we can handle." We are not given more than we can handle because we are God, and as such, we give ourselves nothing we cannot handle. Additionally, as God, we know exactly what we need to grow.

We draw challenges into our experience to help us release our self-imposed barriers and attain self-realization.

Living my exact experiences gave me my gift. We can't fix something that isn't broken, so we need to experience being broken to have the incentive to correct our flawed thinking. Our contracts are our experiences with other people who show us what we are subconsciously already thinking. They help us to build our foundations for strength, and to understand what we need to heal in our minds to recognize our platform for our greatest achievements.

We can view the way things affect us as an indicator of what we are thinking. If we do not like an experience, we need to ask ourselves why we drew that experience to ourselves and what we need to change in our mindset. What do we need to release in our thinking to change our experiences?

By showing us what we are thinking, our contracts become significant. If we lived our lives with no agony, there would be no joy. If there were no darkness, we would not be able to appreciate the light. Each bit of pain makes the laughter all the more pleasant. Thus it is with everything. Our most painful experiences and contracts are the ones we need to fully appreciate the joyful ones. Savor the experience; in it you will understand the workings of your spirit.

~ Exercises ~

Take a look at where you are now. Look at your likes, dislikes, hobbies, work, friends, and foes. Make two columns on a piece of paper and list the people who have had a major influence on who you are today, including the seemingly positive and seemingly negative influences. List the positive and negative in two separate columns.

Look at your list and assess why you determined that some were positive influences and some were negative. How were these experiences validating your preconceived definition of self?

Try to look objectively at the experiences from a standpoint of love. Can you see where you allowed some to affect you negatively and some to affect you positively because of your belief system? Had you not already felt that these statements were true, would you have let them bother you and affect you the way they did?

~ **Bully Victim Dynamic** ~

"He who falls in love with himself will have no rivals."

- Benjamin Franklin

When children in school attack one another, both people involved in the bullying dynamic are suffering from the same form of pain. I dislike using the common terms "bully" and "victim" because they perpetuate the same mindset that needs correcting. The minds of children are extremely malleable, and labeling is one of the most subtle and destructive forms of attack and manipulation.

When we define a child by saying "you are…" we project our own feelings of frustration, anger, fear, and limitation upon the child. It is never a true evaluation of the child we are seeing, but a reflection of our own frustration, anger, fear, and limitation. If we saw the child or other adult in proper perspective, we would see only that he or she is a valuable human being who wants to be accepted and loved.

On her website Lynne Namka, Ph.D., notes that she has also developed an effective way of dealing with anger issues for everyone, including kids. For more information, visit, www.

Angriesout.com. In her article, "Shame and the Disowned Part of Self," she touches on dysfunctional behavior and how it arises from core feelings of guilt and shame by disowning or trying to dissociate parts of ourselves from ourselves. For example, narcissistic people might feel deep down that they can never be good enough and therefore obsess over their appearance in an effort to hide their perceived flaw. Similarly, a bully learns to behave in such a manner to fit in and disguise what he or she feels is a personal flaw. Bullies develop a tough skin to hide their perceived flaw, which might be interpreted as a weakness. The most frightening thing to people who take on the bully role is to be judged as seeming weak or inferior. They therefore display behavior they think will disguise their weakness most effectively by acting physically, emotionally, or socially superior to their victim.

"Shame is a fear-based internal state of being, accompanied by beliefs of being unworthy and basically unlovable. Shame is a primary emotion that conjures up brief, intense painful feelings and a fundamental sense of inadequacy. Shame experiences bring forth beliefs of 'I am a failure' and 'I am bad' which are a threat to the integrity of the self. The perceived deficit of being bad is so humiliating and disgraceful that there is a need to protect and hide the flawed self from others. Fears of being vulnerable, found out, exposed, and further humiliated are paramount. Feelings of shame shut people down so that they can distance from the internal painful state of hopelessness." - Lynne Namka, Ph.D.

Research has also shown that "bullies" have all learned their behavior as a form of defense against feeling rejected, unloved, or not good enough, which stems from within the home. These feelings of being unlovable, flawed, or rejected often surface before the people can even express themselves verbally. The pain of self-perception is therefore so deeply buried that the bully is often in complete denial of any pain, as a form of defense against seeming weak and exposing weakness to anyone. Bullies want to fit in and be seen as worthy of admiration in the eyes of their peers.

All the findings for identifying the components of what creates a bully have one underlying factor: the child who bullies is not getting the positive attention he or she needs and therefore feels a need to bully others to feel accepted.

An extreme example of the bully/victim dynamic is seen in street gangs. When I lived in the Cayman Islands, my car was stolen by a thirteen-year-old member of a street gang. It is not a natural response for people to infringe on others, so there must have been more to the scenario than meets the eye. It would been easy for me to assume that the kid who stole my car just wanted to take it for a joy-ride.

Is it normal behavior for someone who feels safe, secure, and accepted to steal the property of another? Perhaps this child felt he had no other choice than to steal the car. I have no idea why he stole it, but I can imagine a few scenarios.

Let's imagine one in which the boy experienced extreme neglect and abuse at home. Maybe his parents were drug users and there was never enough money or time for them to provide for him properly because of their addiction. The boy met some of his parents' friends who had nice clothes, drove nice cars, and always seemed to have money. The drug-dealing friends of his parents might have seemed like good role models to emulate.

One night, one of his parents' "friends" comes to their home to collect on a drug debt. There is a fight and the friend threatens the boy's parents. The boy is crying and asks the "friend" not to harm his parents. The friend says, "Your parents will be fine if you can get me some money." The boy has no idea how to get the money and the friend says, "Steal a car and bring it to me and your parents' debt will be forgiven."

For a kid who is afraid that his parents will be harmed, stealing a car might be his only perceivable option. If he gets away with the crime, he might decide that he can help his parents more by selling drugs for their friend in his school. This will help Mommy and Daddy stay safe and will also help him to have a sense of belonging and self-worth.

I know nothing about the life of the kid who stole my car, but the scenario I have outlined is much more probable than that he stole it just to go joy-riding. Is the kid a bully or a victim? Is this a situation that requires punishment or rehabilitation? The lines become fuzzy. We can imagine that the drug dealer and the boy's parents also fell into similar circumstances. There comes a point where you become trapped by your circumstances and it is very difficult to escape the negative mindset.

There is a fine line between bully and victim. Both are responses to feeling guilt and shame about self. The perpetrator of the crime of stealing my car would be viewed as exhibiting bullying behavior by stealing the personal property of another. The perpetrator is actually at a disadvantage because our society is focused on punishment rather than rehabilitation. It might seem a bit unorthodox, but the way I see it, the victim is at an advantage, and considering current social norms his or her needs are more likely to be addressed.

We are all equally strong, valuable, and important. There is no inferiority or superiority, only the perception that the two exist. The perception of inferiority or superiority is a false perception based on self-doubt. There are bullies and victims everywhere. At times, most of us take on the roles of playing both. If you've ever said something spiteful or hurtful to someone, ever tried to intimidate someone, or used your power to establish your dominance over another, you have experienced the feelings associated with being a bully. If you have ever had someone do or say something to you that made you react negatively through feelings of fear, shame, unworthiness, or inferiority, you know what it feels like to play the victim.

For bullies to mask the pain they feel inside from neglect, abuse, or unworthiness, they develop a tough exterior so that no one can see how much pain they harbor. We cannot give something that we haven't got. In the bully/victim dynamic, the bully is dishing out pain to others because he or she is suffering from pain, and is afraid of seeming weak, so they exploit a weakness in another person to elevate their own feelings of self-worth. By exploiting another's weakness, the bully's personal pain or weakness is masked through dysfunctional behaviors by being seemingly brave. False bravery born of self-preservation brings the bully a sense of self-worth and the admiration of his or her peers.

The bully is therefore suffering from the pain he or she is trying to mask. Bullies also hurt themselves by trying to make others feel week or inferior: we only do to others what we would expect for ourselves. The bully is actually suffering from a deep-seated pain or dissociation and is increasing his pain through bullying behavior.

I cannot claim to know what prompted Andy to target me on the school bus; however, I do know that he must have been feeling some form of pain in order to dish out the degree of pain that he did. He was no mean, horrid monster. He was a little boy in seventh grade who wanted to establish his social and physical superiority. Had he truly felt that he was superior to me, he would never have wasted his breath trying to prove it. It never would have dawned on me that someone would have considered him fat, but the kid on the bus who stood up for me did, thereby exposing something Andy had been so vehemently trying to disguise through his attacks.

My experience with Andy is one of my greatest gifts, and I am truly grateful for it. Knowing what I know now, I hope that through my healing he will someday find the courage to look within himself, explore his own pain, and find the strength to heal his own mind.

~ Exercises ~

Can you identify a time when you took on the role of the bully through criticism, verbal lashings, physical attack or any other form of aggression? If so, what weakness do you suspect you were trying to hide? Describe in as much detail as possible.

Can you identify a time when you took on the role of the victim? What perceived weakness of yours was being exposed? Describe in as much detail as possible.

~ Thoughts Create Our Experience ~

*"Life is a creative idea; it can only find itself
in changing forms."* - Rabindranath Tagore

We choose our thoughts. Every day, every moment, we are either choosing to live unlimited, loving lives or limited, fearful lives. Our bodies never do anything that our minds don't tell them to do. We can choose to live a life of love or a life of fear. Love is offered through extension and is the recognition of the majesty and unity of everyone. Fear is offered through projection and is the illusion that we are separate and different from everyone.

All feelings that make us feel separate from one another are projections of fear. Anger is the fear of being attacked or weakened; judgment is the fear of being flawed or wrong. Fear is an invention created by the ego, by which we believe we are separate from one another and therefore separate from God. Through a belief in separation, we feel we can be denied love. Think about it. The one thing people fear most is death. What is the fear of death other than the feeling that our creator will stop loving us and we will therefore cease to exist?

We feel two basic emotions; fear and love. Whatever we offer to others is what we receive. If we offer fear, whether in the form of anger, jealousy, judgment, or any other emotion that reinforces our feelings of separation, we feed that part of ourselves. We will be more fearful and feel more separate in the future. When we offer love, we offer harmony and peace to those around us, and in doing so, we feed our own love, increase it in us, and offer peace and love to ourselves.

A typical argument between my husband and me might occur as follows: we have two toddlers, and I take my job of being a full-time mother very seriously and want to provide the most loving, positive atmosphere possible so that they grow up feeling self-confident and secure. I want my kids to know that they are only limited by the scope of their imaginations. Having two toddlers can be very draining, especially if they are being uncooperative and refuse to take a nap in the middle of the afternoon. I become very tired at times and short-tempered. I fear that I am a less effective parent if I lose my cool. Ultimately, I fear that my children will feel unloved if I am less than patient with them, and I condemn myself for losing my patience.

I have a tendency to project my frustration on my husband. He will come home after a long day at work and an hour-long commute, just happy to be home with his family. He'll take off his coat and shoes and give everybody a kiss and a hug. I might then lash out at him for working such long hours and not spending enough time with his kids. I might not even come out and say that I want him to play with his kids or that I need a break, but expect him to read my mind and know what I need.

I project my anger onto him, which he might or might not notice. Whether he notices or not, I then feel guilt for projecting the anger onto him. Without even realizing that the whole scenario is in my mind, I will think he is the one who is angry with me, when it is really my own anger and frustration I feel. I project my anger on to him, then see my reflection as him being angry with me. Eventually, he will get the hint that I am angry for some reason and his fear will then kick into high gear. He will then project his fear in the form of anger back at me because by now he feels he has done something wrong to jeopardize my love for him.

The whole thing could be avoided if I would just give myself the love and permission to become tired and know that I am a good mother whether I become tired or not.

Throughout our lives, we go through experiences that we think are either beneficial or a detrimental to our well-being. It is not the experience itself, but our response to the situation that determines how we view the experience. All events by themselves are neutral; they are just experiences. It is our judgment of the event that determines how it will affect our overall state of mind. If we can keep in mind that it is our reaction to the experiences that makes us feel an emotional response, we can then begin to see that we are in control of our reactions and may choose respond differently.

One of my earliest childhood memories is of my father calling me his "Punkin." As I became verbal and could effectively express my thoughts, I asked my mother why Daddy called me that. She told me it was because he loved me very much and always wanted a Punkin of his very own. I responded by saying that I thought he called me Punkin because I was fat like a pumpkin. She cried when she realized that I had misinterpreted my father's term of endearment, and thought he was teasing me for being fat.

My father never meant for me to interpret "Punkin" to mean that he thought I was physically flawed in any way, yet somewhere along the line I had acquired some deep-seated lack of self-esteem, and "fat" was exactly what I understood "Punkin" to mean. It was not his calling me Punkin that made me feel physically inadequate; Punkin is just a word with no malice in the meaning. I took it upon myself to interpret at a very early nonverbal age that he called me Punkin because he thought I was fat.

The Punkin experience is my first memory of feeling that my body was flawed. I thought I was less perfect than others who were not chubby or fat. I would rather believe that my father thought I was fat than that he loved me tremendously and just wanted to call me Punkin. This experience happened when I was a baby, and through my memory of it, I can see that my thoughts about who I was were developing long before I could express to anyone who I thought I was. By the time my sister was born, three days after my third birthday, my father had long stopped calling me Punkin because of the meaning I had placed upon it.

I also remember playing the "Sooooo Big" game with my mother and feeling that this, too, meant that I was fat. I interpreted the term "big" as meaning "fat," not tall or grown up. I obviously had other experiences that started my programming at an even earlier age, because I must have gotten the idea that I was physically flawed in order to link the Punkin experience and the "Sooooo Big" experience to mean I was fat. The point is, at a very early age I chose to define myself as fat. Had I not already believed this to be true, it would not have affected me the way it did. I would have had pleasant memories of playing with my mother, instead of feeling that the experience was reinforcing my feelings of having a flawed body.

In both of these examples, I chose to interpret a benign experience as something it was not. It was my interpretation of the experience that made me feel that I was fat, not the experience itself. Any rational person would know that my parents were not calling me fat and were just being attentive parents, a simple interaction that could have been interpreted as a positive, esteem-building experience. At a very early age, however, I adopted the belief that I was imperfect and physically flawed.

Because of my self-definition, I chose to interpret most experiences as ones in which I saw myself as physically flawed. When I had an experience wherein someone blatantly told me that I was physically imperfect, I used that experience as validation that my opinion was correct thereby strengthening my belief that my opinion was indeed true. These experiences had a strong impact and I can recall them effortlessly. At a very early age, I was building a case that I was flawed, and each circumstance that validated the belief stuck in my mind as my proof of my "truth."

Had I been able to look at my experiences objectively, I would have seen that I could reject the seeming evaluations of others as false perceptions. I believed their evaluations and judgments to be true; I accepted them wholeheartedly and chose to carry the heavy burden of physical imperfection that translated into extra pounds.

A friend of mine had a miraculous healing experience at the age of six because she did not allow negative thoughts to enter her mind about her physical well being. She had polio and cured herself by not giving the thought any of her energy. She tells her story below:

"When I was six, I had polio. The doctors told me I would never walk or ride a bike. I decided, as a six-year-old that they were not talking about me. They were talking about what happens to others when they have polio. I didn't pay any attention to the words they told me and gave the prediction none of my energy.

The doctors were wrong. I walk, ride, dance, do yoga, and any form of physical exercise I want to do. It took me thirty years to realize how amazing it was to not listen to the doctors' prediction and just carry along with my own life the way I wanted to live it.

My parents were going through a divorce at the time and I found it interesting years later to know that Louise Hay says that polio is caused by thoughts of paralyzing jealousy or a desire to stop someone."

Jan felt paralyzed to stop her parents from breaking up, and that thought manifested in her body as polio. The denial of the thought having any power over her was what cured her of the disease. In both the experiences in my life and in Jan's life, our thoughts created the way we experienced our reality, and it was our thoughts that determined how we responded both physically and emotionally to our situations.

~ **Exercises** ~

Can you identify instances in which you chose to misinterpret an innocent interaction as a negative experience? Describe in as much detail as possible.

Can you identify an illness or health issue you have? If so, identify what the illness does to your body. If you can, write what thoughts you are or were you harboring that may have caused the illness to manifest in your body.

Try to identify what core guilt or separation issues you were projecting onto the situation. Can you see that you chose to interpret the situation in the way you did and use that as validation for your established issues of dissociation and separation?

~ Creating Our Reality ~

*"We are what we think.
All that we are arises with our thoughts.
With our thoughts, we make the world."*
- Gautama Buddha

The power of thought is not yet fully understood. It is not just thinking that something will happen that makes it happen, it is also feeling in our hearts that something is true that makes it happen. If we say we are worthy of making a great salary, but we do not believe it, we will not make a great salary. The good thing about thought is that we can train ourselves to believe whatever we want.

We were trained to believe that we have deficiencies we did not believe we had before entering into this lifetime, and we can train ourselves to believe the opposite of the training that created those thought patterns. Just because we can change our thought patterns does not mean it is easy. It took us our entire lifetime to believe what we do about ourselves. If we do not work on vigorously retraining ourselves, it could take that amount of time to heal our thoughts about ourselves.

Many people have publicly praised the power of positive thinking and how it changed their lives. These people have used visualization, affirmations, and other tools to transform themselves and their lives into something preferable.

To change our minds, we must first recognize destructive thought patterns we believe. Upon identifying the core patterns, we can work on changing them. For example, we might think that we are fat and tell ourselves that we are thin. For me, fatness was not where my negative pattern was rooted; my negative pattern was in my lack of self-love. Telling myself "I am thin" would not have worked because being fat was only a symptom of my lack of self-love. I used my negative self image to further condemn myself. Telling myself "I love myself unconditionally and I am a thin, attractive person." allowed me to accept my body and become thin while not obsessing about my weight.

I saw myself as unworthy of love and therefore attributed it to my weight, not my heart. I eventually became thin after I accepted myself and no longer obsessed over my weight. I had to work on self-love and being worthy of love. For the first time in my life I am accepting myself as I am, and loving what I see. When I look at myself in the mirror now, I see a sexy goddess, not an unlovable fatso. I am the one who previously made the harsh judgments about myself and those harsh judgments took their toll on my self-image.

If you feel great about yourself, people will see you as the self-image you project. Whatever you feel about yourself is projected in your energy. Whatever you think about yourself, people will think about you. I am slimmer now than I used to be, but it is because my self-image has changed and my physical image now corresponds with my new thoughts about who I am.

I used to believe that I am the person I am because of experiences I had. I believed that I was a product of my experience, and other people identified traits in me that I accepted as my truth or I rejected as false. I believed that my experiences with others, good and bad, had more to do with who I was or who they were than who I thought I was. Until recently, I had not considered the opposite: that I had the thought about who I am and then the experience followed.

The concept of our thoughts being creative, leads me to conclude the following: If we are created in the image of God, God is therefore a creator. God dwells in us and therefore we must also be creators. If God is a creator and we are in the image of God, we create our own reality. Our creative capacity is what is meant by free will. We choose the experiences we desire, and thus bring them to ourselves. Because we are constantly creating our own reality, we use our imaginations to create whatever we desire.

If we think of God as an idea, we can see that we too are ideas. We then have the ability to create an idea and draw the experience of our creation (idea) to us. We therefore experience a universe of our own creation.

If we focus on negativity and what we do not want in our lives, we draw into our lives what we do not want. My whole life, I focused on my physical "flaw" and therefore drew experiences that validated that point of view.

Since God is good, there is always a positive side to every seemingly negative experience. The positive side of my experiences was that, had I viewed them as my own creation,

I could have seen that all I needed to do was change my perspective and my experience would change. If I experienced my body as a vehicle of pleasure and happiness, as a tool or vessel to use in understanding my divinity, my experience would have been of a much different nature.

I am now and have always been the creator of my experience, and by experiencing myself in a positive light, I now draw positive experiences to myself. If I focus on the outcomes that I view as positive, I draw positive experiences to me. When I have an experience that can be interpreted as negative, I view it in a positive light because it is showing me something I can address within that I had not addressed before, which will lead to greater love and awareness.

The creative nature of thought brings me back to judgment and criticism. When we judge, we are focusing on things that we view in the negative. If our energy is spent on negativity, negativity is what we draw to ourselves. Consider your thoughts to be money. Money is the way we exchange energy in our modern cultures, and is the way we value things. It is not the green paper and the little disks that we cherish, but the things we can buy with them.

Consider this: Each idea you have is a dollar. The more time and energy you invest in that particular idea, the more dollars you have to buy that particular idea, whether it's a car, house, relationship, the way you see yourself, or whatever it may be. If I keep telling myself that I'm worthless and nobody will ever love me, I'm investing my energy in that idea. Eventually, after telling myself enough times that I'm unworthy of being loved, I will draw experiences that validate that point of view, because in an unbiased universe, lack of love must be what I want, since I focus all my energy on it. If, on the other hand, I focus on giving everything I have to others and spreading my own love to the far reaches of the planet, I will then reap the rewards of my thoughts. I will draw so much love to myself that I can't help but give it away more and more, creating an endless cycle.

You see, it happens in both ways. If I perceive myself as unworthy of being loved, my experiences will validate that point of view, which will make me believe even more that I am unworthy of being loved, and so on. The cycle will continue until it is broken by a radical change in perception. The person will not physically change; the mind has to change and be re-programmed in order to see positive results. The mind must change first, then the creative forces of the mind will be witnessed in the physical realm.

Let's say that I can indeed create my own universe and I perceive myself as being flawed, limited, or lacking something. Because of my belief system, my world will reflect my beliefs. If I draw these experiences to me, and I do not gain pleasure and happiness from my experiences, I need to recognize that I created them, and therefore I can change my outlook and the way I experience my world. We have the thought first, then the experience follows. It is therefore very important that we claim responsibility for our own thoughts as well as our actions, because the world we experience is a product of our thoughts. Gaining control over your thoughts is the key to gaining control over your destiny. Allow yourself to think only about what you want in your life, not what you don't want. When you know what you want, allow your positive thoughts to guide your actions, and trust your positive thoughts to steer you toward your greater good.

Everything we experience is in our lives because we desired it. The degree that our desires are made manifest in our lives is equivalent to the amount of energy we give any thought or idea. We mistakenly believe that our grievances are the effect of a cause outside ourselves. We think that because of outside influences, we are given a set of circumstances and we are products of our environment or upbringing. We are products of our own thoughts, and whatever thoughts we choose to give our energy to will produce our experience.

Long before my grandmother ever told me that I couldn't be a singer if I wasn't skinny, I believed that if I were not skinny, I couldn't be a singer. The same thing happened with the ballet teacher. I already believed that I was fat before she told me I was. The same thing happened with Andy.

The context was the gift. Through a spattering of experiences like playing the "So Big" game with my mother, and my father calling me Punkin, I mistakenly thought my parents were telling me I was fat. Somewhere else, I must have come to the conclusion that being fat was bad. I independently drew the conclusion that I was fat and therefore bad but I did not have anything concrete in which to understand what I had been thinking. Since my thoughts revolved around what I thought was lacking, I was able to identify that lack, and name it through my painful experiences.

One way of looking at our experiences is that they give us validation for what we are already thinking. Another way of looking at them is that they offer us the context to understand the content of our thinking. Since our thoughts create our experiences, we experience both validation and context for them. If we do not like the experience, we need to look into it to understand why and find what we need to correct in our thinking to have a more positive experience in the future. The more an experience affects us—the angrier, more depressed, helpless, desperate, or vulnerable we feel—the greater the incentive to correct that part of our thinking because it will only return in another form until we address the issues that manifest the experiences. Our experiences would not affect us negatively or cause pain if we didn't believe they were true in the first place.

I had an experience that very clearly showed me how I create my experience and exactly how powerful my mind is. I entered a speech competition. I thought I wanted to win and joined a second club with the hopes that doing so would increase my chances of winning. The way the competition works in Toastmasters is that you first compete at the club level against three or four of your fellow club members. There are four or five clubs in an area, so the next level is Area, then Division, and so on, until you reach the International level.

In the second club I joined, there was a guy named Ryan who, at eight years old, won a public speaking championship for 4H at the state level, talking about LEGOs. Even before joining the other club, I was a bit intimidated by the guy and viewed him as the one speaker to whom I might lose in competition. Why shouldn't I be intimidated? At the time of the speech competition, he was about twenty-six and had been a public speaker for about twenty years. Additionally, in the last contest he entered, he went all the way to the District-level competition, which means that of the 3,500 people who entered the competition in the district, he was in the top five.

In preparing for my club competition where I was to compete against him, I concerned myself with two things: I wanted to make an impression on as many people as possible, and I feared that I might lose the contest to Ryan. Sure enough, I did make an impression on many people who attended the competition, and sure enough, I came in second to Ryan.

That was okay, though, because I still had the other club that I would be competing in, and even though the club was four times the size of the club I was in with Ryan, I had no fears about winning that one. Sure enough, I placed first in that contest and won the opportunity to compete at the Area level, where I would again compete against Ryan.

In preparing for the Area level competition, the first concern I had was about losing to Ryan, the second was that I was told that a certain judge who would be judging my speech was notorious for not understanding the types of speeches I give. I was concerned that the judge would not "get it," so I spent hours improving and simplifying my speech in hopes that the judge would understand and not give me a low mark because he didn't understand the speech. The change, I thought, would then allow me to come in first, ahead of Ryan.

The title of my speech was "Whatever Doesn't Kill you Only Makes you Stronger." I talked about how we draw certain experiences to ourselves through our thoughts. I used my three favorite examples: my grandmother, my ballet teacher, and Andy. I explained to the audience that I had the thoughts first and that I drew the experiences to myself in order to provide myself the context to understand what I had been thinking.

I then told them how they could change their thoughts and focus on positive things in order to filter out negative experiences, and thereby draw more positive experiences to themselves. I delivered the speech with poise and purpose; my gestures were right on; my eye contact was perfect. I knew the speech was filled with great content, that it was the best damn speech I had ever delivered.

Afterward, I was getting thumbs up all over, and many people told me that they were affected by my words. Then the Area governor stood up and said, "The person who will represent Area forty eight in the event that the winner can not be present is Kerri Kannan." What? I couldn't believe it; I didn't win.

A few very interesting things happened next. First, Ryan won. The judge I had concerned myself about came up to me and said, "You know, your stories were good, but I just didn't get it." Also, a line of people waited to talk to me and tell me what a great impact I made on them with the speech.

It took an hour of feeling sorry for myself before it hit me: I had drawn to myself the exact outcome that I had been focusing on. I thought I was focused on winning because I was thinking about not wanting to lose to Ryan and not wanting that judge to miss the point. The only thing I focused on in the positive was that I wanted to affect as many people as possible, and that happened too.

I tell this story to illustrate two points: First, we do indeed draw to ourselves the exact experiences that we focus our thoughts on, and our minds are very powerful; second, the universe is unbiased and nonjudgmental. It will not negate the energy of our focus. If we focus on what we do not want, we will draw that experience to ourselves. If we focus on what we do want, we will draw that experience to ourselves. We need always to think in the positive. Positive thinking will bring us positive results.

The illustration below shows how our thinking influences the way we perceive the world.

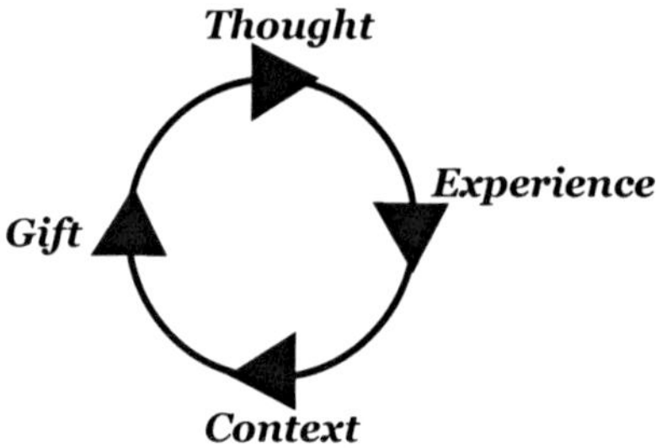

• We have a Thought.
• We then have an Experience we use to understand or validate our thoughts.
• The experience provides us with Context to understand what we are thinking.
• The context provides us with a Gift to understand what we are thinking.
• If we do not like our experiences, we need to change our thoughts. When we change our thoughts, we change the way we experience the world.
• Then the cycle continues.

~ **Exercises** ~

What is your internal tape recorder playing? List some of your daily thoughts about yourself and your experiences. Try to be as honest with yourself as possible. Take a day or two and monitor your thoughts. You might be surprised at what you are thinking.

From the thoughts you are telling yourself, can you see why your life is the way it is? Being the creator of your experience through your thoughts, what type of life are you creating for yourself?

Look at your observations about your thoughts. Do you like the experiences you are drawing to yourself? If not, what are you telling yourself that you need to change in your thinking to change your experience?

~ **Listening and Going Within** ~

"For whereas the mind works in possibilities, the intuitions work in actualities, and what you intuitively desire, that is possible to you. Whereas what you mentally or 'consciously' desire is nine times out of ten impossible; hitch your wagon to a star, or you will just stay where you are."

- D. H. Lawrence

The universe communicates with us in several ways: it communicates through "coincidences," inner urges, gut feelings, nudges or pangs, when we suddenly think about people we don't usually think about, through songs that remind us of other people, through flash images, dreams, or having someone pop into our heads when we just can't shake the thought of that person. The most important thing we can do when trying to make a decision is to listen to our inner voice. Our lives stay on track when we listen to our gut feelings. The more you listen, the more easily things will fall into place for you and the more easily you will see your goals and realize your dreams.

We have all been equipped with an inner guide or voice to help us to know the right decisions to make. We know the voice of our guides or of God by the messages we receive. These messages are always persistent, never judgmental, never fear based, and always love based.

I have had several experiences where I was thinking about someone and my intuition was right on. A few months after I got married, the thought raced through my head to ask my husband when the last time was that he spoke to his friend Dave. We hadn't heard from him in at least six months, and in a matter of seconds, the phone rang. Dave was on the other end.

Another experience that had was thinking of a friend who had cancer. My stepmother died of cancer about five years before, and I knew that she had a friendly relationship with a woman named Harlin and her husband Steven. He was a member of a community service organization that held its meetings in my father's restaurant, so I saw him often. He was always very nice to me in the restaurant and I always liked his warm, friendly presence.

Also, I went to high school with one of his sons. I was never close to the son but always thought he was a nice guy. When I started thinking about the family, I wasn't sure why. Was I thinking about Benjamin, the guy I went to school with, or was I thinking about Steven, or was it the family in general? I knew that Steven had also been sick in the past; however, the last time I had heard about his health was about four years prior, after he had gone into remission. I couldn't stop thinking about this family, so I sent off an e-mail to Benjamin telling him that I was thinking about his family and hoped his father was doing well.

I visited my father the next weekend, and when I got there, phoned Harlin to tell her I was thinking about her and her family. I found out that Steven had had a recurrence and was not doing well. I gave Harlin the number of a spiritual healer I knew of and let her know that she, Steven, and the family were in my thoughts.

I thought of the family on an almost constant basis, and a few months later, I ran into Harlin at my father's restaurant. When I saw Harlin, I asked her where Steven was and she said that he had died three weeks earlier. I later found out that instead of a funeral, they had a Celebration of Life, and hundreds of people attended the "graduation party."

I don't know why I kept thinking about the family. Perhaps it was just to let them know I was thinking about them, or so that I would have knowledge of their "Celebration of Life," or so I could record the experience in this book. No matter the reason, the experience is significant. I don't know how the family views death but its members inspired me. Now I know I want my last hoorah also to be a Celebration of Life.

I know that through our minds we are all connected. All we need do is just listen and we will hear each other's call. When I think about Steven I don't feel an absence of his presence, I feel more of a peaceful calm and the ever-friendly warm presence I grew to know a long time ago.

Listening to your inner promptings is also useful when trying to decide where to go in life. Listening to our own internal guidance system will keep us on course. The better you listen to your intuitions, the quicker you will find the path of least resistance and your life purpose.

Fulfilling your part in the universal puzzle will improve your life. If someone tries to keep you from listening to the dictates of your heart, that person is doing so out of fear and an effort to control, not love. It is okay to try to advise someone, but it is not okay to impose your views on another merely because you don't understand why he or she must do things his or her own way. Do not let fear stop you from accomplishing your purpose. Fear is the illusion that points in the opposite direction from love. It is the voice of self doubt. Fear is the feeling you have when you have one foot on the gas and one foot on the brake. Take your foot off the brake and go for it.

Movement toward fulfillment of your dreams will improve your relationships with yourself and the rest of humanity. I have found that the more I learn and grow, the more confident and self-assured I become. The more I honor myself by listening to my inner dictates, the happier I become, which rubs off on everyone around me. The better I feel about myself, the better everyone around me feels about themselves, which rubs off on their loved ones. Every time we communicate, we are teaching lessons and affirming our beliefs about ourselves. The more encounters we have with others, the more we teach our beliefs.

We can hear our inner promptings best when we are quiet and listen to our hearts through meditation, journaling, or finding our inner stillness.

When my brother came home and suggested that I move to Minnesota, my internal promptings convinced me to move there instead of North Carolina. My decision was not based on any deductive reasoning or rational conclusions, it was all based on intuition. I eventually gave in to my internal dictates and told everyone that I decided to move to Minnesota to establish a better relationship with my brother. I thought if I told anyone I was moving there because the voice inside me said I was going to meet my husband there, I would be taken for psychiatric evaluation.

On February 12, 1997 I arrived in St. Paul, Minnesota, and on February 13 I met my future husband. Before the anniversary of our third month together, we knew that we would be getting married. My intuition guided me in my time of uncertainty.

After I realized my purpose, I knew I needed to improve my speaking skills if I was to effectively deliver my message. I thought Toastmasters could help me focus my message and give me the confidence I needed to deliver it effectively. I visited one Toastmasters meeting in October and didn't attend again for several months. "Coincidentally," I kept bumping into the man who led the meeting I attended. Because I kept seeing him, the thought of joining Toastmasters remained fresh in my mind. The funny thing is, since I joined Toastmasters, I haven't bumped into him once. The internal prompting was all I needed to join, and I believe that I kept seeing that man because joining Toastmasters was something I needed to do.

We are all connected, and this is also scientifically evidenced through studies of the Morphic Field by British scientist Rupert Sheldrake. I have been obsessed with the workings of the field, wherein we can tap into the thoughts of others and connect with them from thousands of miles away. Because I wanted to experience unity with all, I had been praying about experiencing the field for a while. I wanted to experience the constant feeling of love and recognizing on a conscious level that there is no separation, that we are all truly united. As with most of my experiences of late, I am finding that all I need to do is ask the question and it is answered.

The workings of the field are evident through my experience of thinking about Steven and Harlin's family; however, sometimes I have found that if we listen, we will receive answers to our questions at precisely the moments we need them. We don't always receive our answers from an expected source, but since we are all connected through the field, our answers may come from any source. I've been much more aware lately of the answers to my questions and have had a few experiences that seem to be evidence that we are all one and intimately interconnected.

One day when I was feeling particularly unsure about my ability to affect people deeply, I sent an e-mail to a writer friend, asking him if he thought my book would be good. At first he responded by saying, "Good to me is different from most people, and I'm not ducking the question. Most writers worry about selling a lot of copies. I don't see the world of publishing that way. If you write the book faithfully, to your heart and inner eye, then the universe is changed appropriately, and it may sell a lot, but that's never been my concern." This was not the response I wanted, so I worded the question differently by saying, "Your response helps to a point, but you still ducked the question. Do you think it will be good? Not will it sell, do you think it will be good? Do you think people will benefit from my thoughts put into words and remember who they are through my words? Do you think I have within me the capacity to help people heal their self-images and recognize themselves as perfect expressions of beauty and divinity? Do you think it will speak to people's souls? Do you think the world will be a better place because of my contribution?"

To this he responded, "Write it for one person, the person who most needs to hear it, not someone you've ever met, and make yourself understood to that one person alone, just that one, and it will be good."

My friend's response was what I was looking for, yet I didn't realize it was the answer I was seeking. I had one of those "unusual coincidences" that just seems too perfectly timed and too specific to my question to be a coincidence.

The next day, I checked my e-mail; in my inbox was a correspondence from a woman who previously found my workbook online and was helped by its message. During a prior correspondence, she told me about neighbors who were having issues with alcoholism and that she was going to direct them to my website because she thought it would be beneficial to them.

The day after I asked my friend if he thought I could reach people, the same woman sent me a message: "Just wanted to let you know that my alcoholic neighbor has just checked in to detox! His girlfriend told me yesterday and mentioned your article as being the thing that helped him to take the step. I thought you might like to know. Keep doing what you're doing!"

The validation from this woman I'd never met was the validation I had been looking for when I posed the question to my friend. Although he could validate me to a point, he could not give me the concrete answers I wanted. The message telling me that my work helped someone make the decision to finally go into a rehabilitation program was the best answer I could have possibly received in my moment of self-doubt. Through this news I received my validation.

Another way of listening to your inner promptings is to pay attention to your dreams. When we sleep, our minds work on problems or we gain insight that we would not normally be tuned in to during our waking hours. Keep a dream diary. Write down your dreams upon awakening, and eventually you will see a pattern.

If you are not the type of person who will write down the dream when you wake, don't worry. I usually don't have the luxury of having the time to write down my dreams upon awakening because my children usually wake me. Instead, pay attention to the dreams you can remember throughout the day. The dreams that we can easily recall are the ones we are supposed to remember, and these will help us gain insight into the workings of our subconscious.

One of my most significant spiritual releases came to me in the form of a dream. I thought about the healing dream when I hugged Andy for months because the content of it was so powerful. Because of the dream, I was finally able to forgive Andy and thank him for delivering my experience with him on the school bus.

We all are guided. When we listen to our inner voice, we are being guided. When we go against our internal guidance we run into problems. If we continue to ignore our inner voice, we usually end up in crisis and have no choice but to listen to our internal dictates.

We can decide not to, but life will be much more difficult and not nearly as rewarding if we do. The worst thing to do is to make a decision based on fear or because we are trying to please someone else. We have these fears because we are afraid of the unknown or because we think people will not be accepting of our decisions. We stay in bad relationships and dead-end jobs because we believe a known entity is better than an unknown entity. We would rather live in an unfavorable situation than face the unknown.

Listen to your guidance, inner promptings, coincidences, and spontaneous insights, and they will lead you in the right direction when you come to the multi-pronged fork in the road. They whisper in your ear in order to keep you on track in fulfilling your life contract. You can tell the difference between your ego and your true inner voice by the characteristics of love. Your inner guidance will always nudge you in a positive, loving way. If the voice of judgment is what you hear, you can bet that it's your ego talking. Step boldly in the direction of love and don't give any of your power over to fear.

Listening is the key to avoiding the big hurdles in the road. Once you tune in to what your intuition and promptings are trying to tell you, you will notice that things fall into place more easily. Listen to your inner promptings, they can make all the difference in the world.

~ Exercises ~

The universe is constantly communicating with us to keep us on course. How has the universe communicated with you? Describe any promptings, nudges, coincidences, psychic experiences, or other such experiences.

Has there ever been anything you tried to avoid and were finally forced into a situation where you had no choice but to listen to your internal dictates? What were the trying to tell you?

What did this or these experiences tell you about your internal guidance?

Have you ever been in a situation in which you asked the opinion of another and went against the dictates of your conscience? How did this turn out, and what if anything would you have done differently?

____

____

____

____

____

____

____

____

____

____

____

____

____

____

____

~ Virtue of Longing ~

"Feeling and longing are the motive forces behind all human endeavor and human creations."

- Albert Einstein

The limitations I find myself thinking about these days have less to do with believing I can or cannot be the person I want to be and more of wanting to experience more of a cosmic, all-encompassing love for everyone and everything. I am getting there, but I do not always feel in tune with my God center. I still allow things to bother me, but merely having the awareness that I wish to overcome my obstacles and feel more connected with all is a step in the right direction. I am consciously aware of this goal, and therefore am feeling guided experiences that will help me fulfill my desire.

I have found that longing and pain are wonderful tools. The greater the degree of longing for something, the closer we are to experiencing solutions to our longing. These longings are not things that I usually share with others because they are very personal and spiritual experiences for me. Since I have been longing for a more intimate level of experiencing all, I have been having more psychic and telepathic experiences. I have even been able to physically feel loved ones around me even though they may be hundreds or thousands of miles away. It is almost as if my longings have triggered physical experiences of love and communication but the communications are on a psychic rather than a physical level.

Telepathic and empathic communication is an answer from the universe to a limiting belief I have; that I am limited to physically experiencing love and intimacy through my physical body. The lessons learned through these experiences are there to show me that separation does not exist. This experience is the inverse of what seems obvious and natural to most people, considering that the bulk of our experience here on Earth is in the physical realm. I now know that I can experience anyone I care about merely by thinking about that person and I can feel that presence all around me whenever I think about the person.

Shortly after having the desire to experience all, I had a few telepathic experiences that showed me exactly how to tap into the field.   The field connects us all regardless of space and time, merely through my thoughts. The first experience came after contacting a friend I hadn't seen in seven years. Right before I moved to Minneapolis, I had been dating a man named Joshuah. I cared for Joshuah very deeply; however, Joshuah was about twenty years my senior, had a son who was four years younger than I, and could not give me what I wanted most, children.

Through the years, I had often thought about Joshuah and even tried to contact him a few times, but I could never find him.

One day, I picked from my bookshelf a book someone gave me several years back, and Joshuah's business card dropped from the book. I immediately did an Internet search and found him. Since contacting him, there have been times when I have felt his presence almost constantly. I can feel that he is thinking about me because I can feel him around me all the time. We are now very close friends, and I understand what he means when he says that we can all experience loving others without infringing on their daily lives or their daily consciousness.

I also recognize that, through the years, during the times I could not get him out of my head, he was also thinking about me. The energy has always been the same; however, I now recognize it as the subtle thought waves we exchange through our mutual affection for each other.

There is energy in thought; thought waves are measured as electromagnetic waves. Thought waves are subtle and gentle, yet we can all tap into their energies if we pay attention. Thought is how we communicate. We may be fortunate enough to have a telephone nearby or be in the same room as the person we are communicating with most of the time; however, if we are not, we can still communicate with each other on a more subtle, yet no less effective level.

We are all aspects of God and our minds are linked to the mind of God, connected to each other as one mind. Because we all share the mind of God and God transcends everything, all we need to do is think about someone and we are already in the person's presence.

At a conference last year, I had the pleasure of forming a friendship with a person who was invited to give a speech. He sat at my table for the luncheon and we hit it off. Several weeks later, we were chatting online, and he made a comment I took offense to. His comment was something like, "I've always liked redheads because they are much more passionate than blonds or brunettes." Being a natural blond, I've heard my share of dumb-blond jokes. I've never taken offense to them because I don't generally question my own intelligence but when being questioned about my passion, I had to retort with a quick and witty comment that would end this line of commentary and let him know that one can't judge a woman by her hair color. I told him that an old boyfriend once told me that I was a "passion powerhouse." This statement is not something that strikes me as being terribly provocative because the comment was made several years ago and I have mentioned it now and again. I said it, we changed the subject, and I thought nothing more of it.

Sometimes I have a hard time sleeping when my husband is not in bed with me. He survives on very little sleep and often will work until way past midnight. By the end of the day I'm usually pooped, and often, when the children are ready for bed, I am too.

That night, I woke up at 1:00 or so. I had a very hard time getting back to sleep, not because my husband was not there, but because of the thoughts that kept running through my mind based on the comment I made to my friend. I just kept thinking about the comment, but it was as if it were from his point of view, not mine.

I had no idea that my friend liked to write romance novels for a hobby. The next morning, I checked my e-mail, and saw that during the same time when I was trying to get back to sleep, my friend was writing portion of a romance novel he had been working on relating to my comment.

Some might say it is mere coincidence that I was having the same thoughts he was having at the same time and he sent them to me. I don't believe in coincidence. I believe that I was able to access his thoughts through the morphic field and that since I was the primary focus of his thoughts he was actually transmitting them to me while he was writing. We communicated telepathically, using the morphic field. What was really happening was that he was up thinking about the comment and I was "tuning in" to his thoughts in my relaxed state.

The third experience relating to the morphic field happened early one weekend morning when my husband couldn't sleep anymore and decided to go out for a walk. About half an hour after he left, I felt a strong emotional surge that brought me to sobbing tears. I feel my emotions very deeply, and if something is going on in my life, my feelings sometimes become so intense that I need to cry for a while in order to have a release.

After about thirty minutes of sobbing, it started to dissipate and I was able to go back to sleep. When my husband got home, he said to me, "Were you calling me back? About a half hour into my walk, I felt like you were calling me back to you." I didn't want to admit it to him at the time, because it freaked me out a little that he could read my mind like that but that's exactly what I was doing. I was calling for love, and he was the nearest person who could give me that love. He tapped into my thoughts through the field, and picked up on my message.

I had all of these experiences because I longed to experience more of a connection with all. The morphic field is our connection with all; it is the direct line to God. Longing and the desire to experience things differently are good things. Through the longing, our creative energies find ways of resolving the conflict that we perceive and show us answers that we might not have dreamed we were capable of experiencing.

Through my own longing, I have become more aware that I am not separated from my friends and loved ones, even though it may seem that they are not in my presence. Had I not experienced the longing, I would not have experienced the answer to it and the knowledge that we are already connected.

~ Exercises ~

Are there any instances in which your longings or yearnings have stretched you to have experiences you had not had before the longing presented itself? How have these experiences stretched the boundaries of your mind and shown you a new perspective on your life?

____

____

____

____

____

____

~ **Forgiveness** ~

*"The ineffable joy of forgiving and being forgiven forms
an ecstasy that might well arouse the envy of the gods."*
                                        - Elbert Hubbard

One morning, I brought my daughter to school and found out that they had a one-hour delay because of a power outage. I went to the supermarket and picked up a few things before I had to bring her back to school. I was curious about whether they had regained power, so I flipped through the radio stations to find out. I came across a show that one of my closest friends quotes all the time, yet I had never heard radio personality. Thinking that listening might be enlightening, I decided to just drive to the school and listen to the show.

A woman called in and asked the host about forgiveness. Before she could even ask the question, the host began a dissertation about how these days, forgiveness was too loose a term and was looked at as a way to feel good about oneself by letting someone else off the hook. She listed the following requirements a person must meet before being forgiven:

• The person needs to apologize and feel truly remorseful for committing the offense in the first place.

• The person needs to claim responsibility for hurting the person who would do the forgiving.

• The person needs to make a promise never to commit the offending or hurtful behavior again.

• The person need to ask forgiveness of the person who would do the forgiving.

The person who would be forgiven must meet all requirements and only then should forgiveness be considered. The show host also stated that unless the person being forgiven met all of those requirements, forgiveness should not be given.

When the caller asked if she should forgive the offending person for her own peace of mind, to feel good herself, the "Good Doctor" vehemently defended her position, going on to say, "Why should you forgive someone unless he or she has met all of these requirements? So the offending party can feel good about himself or herself and you can go on hurting? I just told you, unless they have met all four of my requirements, that person should not be forgiven. Forgiveness is not a 'feel-good' thing, it must be carefully and seriously considered. If you want to feel good, have a glass of wine, and disallow this loser to create any more evil in your life. Just shut the person out and do not allow this person back in. You have no room for that person in your life."

The caller then asked her to define "forgiveness." She skirted the question by saying that it has been defined as a "feel-good" remedy and implied that it was a completely bogus ideology and served no purpose in her life.

I'm sure the doctor feels very strongly that forgiveness is a very serious matter and something to be reserved only for the truly remorseful, but what if the offender doesn't realize he or she did anything wrong? What if the offender was acting on stimulus from the past and was responding to the situation in question in accordance with his or her unique past experience? Maybe the offending person subconsciously thought that he or she was in danger of being hurt, and responded to the situation the way they did as a defense mechanism. Unfortunately, the millions of people in the radio personality's audience are gaining nothing from this type of input. We tend to think that if people have a Ph.D. after their names, they know all and we must blindly follow their advice. This is not true. It is fine to ask anyone for advice, but if it doesn't ring true for you, listen to the dictates of your own heart. The caller wanted to forgive, and just needed the blessing of the "Good Doctor."

I could tell from the tone in the caller's voice and the way she just said, "Uh-huh, uh-huh" after the doctor lit into her on the topic of forgiveness, that she didn't feel good about the "expert" advice she had been given. The caller wanted to reach a point of personal peace, yet was not sure whether she should hold a grudge and hold onto the pain, or free herself from the emotional hold the experience had on her. The doctor did her a great disservice by telling her not to forgive the other person.

The doctor is in need of receiving some forgiveness herself. She is either unable to forgive someone for something she feels has been done to her, or she has not been forgiven for something she has done. Until the doctor heals that part of herself, she will feel the need to separate herself from the rest of the world by keeping her grievances alive. She will continue to give faulty advice to the millions of listeners who view her as an authority in relationship matters, and she will further separate herself from her own forgiveness and the healing of her own buried pain.

It is impossible to forgive someone if we feel we have been caused real harm. We can say we forgive a person, but if we feel in our hearts that we have been betrayed or if we feel mistrust of that person, we have not truly forgiven. This is why it is so important to recognize how our most painful experiences are our greatest gifts. If we can truly recognize this, we can see that they are our platform for strength.

The ecstatic state I experienced upon recognizing that my painful experiences were my greatest gifts was the result of forgiveness. I have experienced this blissful state only twice. The first was after recognizing that my life purpose was the opposite of what I perceived to be my grievances. I understood that I had self-imposed limitations that I subconsciously believed to be the difference between me and everybody else. I disliked my body, and it was this distinction that I thought separated me from my fellow humans and God. This thought was not conscious until I was able to forgive some of those I thought had hurt me. I did not recognize that separation is what I was experiencing in my thoughts, actions, and emotional state of mind.

These are some examples of what forgiveness is not:
• Claiming to forgive another out of a feeling of superiority or self-righteousness.
• Claiming to forgive another, yet holding on to lingering feelings of betrayal and pain.

• Claiming to forgive another while belittling that person to others.

• Claiming to forgive, yet revisiting the past as a reminder of the pain he or she caused you.

These are some examples of forgiveness:

• Absolving the perpetrator of all responsibility for making you feel badly.

• Understanding that people act from their own experience and you are reflecting back to them something they want to dissociate within themselves.

• Understanding that no one could ever hurt you because you are an eternal being, incapable of being harmed.

• Understanding that anyone who delivers a painful experience to you is only showing you a portion of your thinking that needs to be corrected or healed.

Painful experiences can not be avoided. The key to forgiveness is identifying with the pain in the person who we feel has hurt us so we can see why they act the way they do.

Ever since she was a little girl, Ann Marie has had difficulty sustaining loving and nurturing relationships with men which traces back to an experience she had with her father. Ann Marie was born the fourth child in a family of five children and was the only girl. When she was little, she had a very special connection with her father. He used to cuddle and nuzzle her, and she was the bright spot in his life. Ann Marie's mother was emotionally abusive, particularly to Ann Marie's father, and to Ann Marie because of the close relationship she had with him.Anne Marie's mother also hated her in-laws, and when things got bad at home, Ann Marie's father went to his mother's house where he knew he would not be bothered by his wife.

When Ann Marie was small, she would go with her older brother, mother, and father to the supermarket every week to get the groceries. When Ann Marie was four years old, her father started the habit of getting her a Little Golden Book each time they went to the market. The day he bought her the fourth book, Ann Marie's mother said to him, "You are always buying that child books, and we don't even have enough money to buy me a new dress!" That was the last book Ann Marie ever got.

When Ann Marie was six and her father and mother were in the throes of one of their arguments, her father took her with him to his mother's house where they spent the entire day. Ann Marie didn't know what time it was when they returned, but it was dark out. Ann Marie's mother took her into the bathroom, gave her a bath and then proceeded to beat Ann Marie with a hairbrush. She interrogated the little girl, screaming, "Why did you stay out so late? Why didn't you come home earlier?" With each question, the mother struck the child with the hairbrush.

Ann Marie stood there being beaten in the bathtub, feeling like her arm would be pulled out of its socket because the bathtub was so slippery, saying, "I'm sorry. I couldn't leave. I don't know how to drive. I'm sorry. I didn't mean it," over and over again.

She came out of the bathroom with welts all over her body and passed by the kitchen to see her father sitting and reading the newspaper as if nothing had happened.

Ann Marie never had a relationship with her father after that, because he did not stand up to his wife when she was taking out her anger with him on the wrong person. The once-close relationship became no relationship with her father, because when she needed protection, he completely ignored her.

As a child, Ann Marie could not see that her father was being abused too. When her father refused to stand up to his wife for himself and his child, he also chose to relinquish his most cherished relationship.

Years later, when Ann Marie entered counseling, her therapist asked why she never talked about her father. She said she didn't because she had no a relationship with him. Later she repeated the pattern of entering relationships with men who were emotionally unavailable. Her whole life, she has been subconsciously trying to heal that relationship with her father by repeating the same pattern of neglect and abuse in her relationships. Until she forgives her father, she will keep looking for acceptance from men who are emotionally unavailable to her. She needs to heal her thinking and understand that her father never intended to hurt her, before she will heal her thinking and ultimately have a healthy, fulfilling, mutually supportive relationship.

Forgiveness is the full recognition that the other person never hurt you to begin with. He or she was a vehicle for you to experience something you had drawn to yourself. The person was fulfilling his or her part of a contract that you carefully planned before this lifetime. We all come here to learn certain lessons, and we make contracts with certain spirits to help us fulfill those contracts. It is important for us to live our lives to the fullest because we are each a part of one another's contracts. Everyone is depending on everyone else.

We cannot be weakened by attack; neither can we weaken another through our own attack. Self-attack is useless because all attack is giving in to the illusion that we can be weakened. If we hold positive thoughts, we allow ourselves to access our infinite divine power.

Everything we do is a choice; from brushing our teeth to paying the bills to feeding ourselves, these are all choices. We also have the power to choose our moods; our moods do not choose us. We can choose to exhibit separation and aggression toward our fellow humans by cutting them off on the highway or not letting them in when they have their blinkers on. We can also choose to allow them to merge, and in doing so, offer ourselves a more peaceful existence.

We can also choose to accept our perceived imperfections as a part of ourselves, and in doing so, offer ourselves love and forgiveness for believing that those thoughts were true. We can choose to believe negative thoughts about ourselves or we can choose to believe only positive, loving thoughts. In choosing positive, loving thoughts, we allow ourselves to claim our power and our birthright.

Once we see that the negativity is an illusion that we have created based on other people's false perceptions about themselves, we can forgive them and actually thank them for showing us our gifts to humanity. The people who have seemingly hurt us are just as misguided as we are, and our forgiveness of them helps them forgive themselves. You don't have to physically tell the people who hurt you that you forgive them, because we share the same mind or essence of spirit, but if you feel compelled, tell them. If you forgive them in your heart, that forgiveness will be recognized in our collective consciousness, and it will be understood.

After I gave the "Trash that Borrowed Cloak" speech and was finally able to forgive Andy, I felt all my animosity melt away. I was left with a feeling of pure love and bliss. I could not harbor negative feelings for Andy because I knew in my heart that, long ago, he had volunteered to bring this lesson for me to recognize my own negative thoughts and feelings of inadequacy. He brought me the gift of context.

There is no death; there is no pain; there is no weakness; there is only love, eternal and infinite. Forgiveness is the key to understanding. You can only forgive someone you perceive has attacked you, and because we are all infinite and limitless, forgiveness is the most natural thing, because what you are forgiving is an illusion.

If you refuse to forgive someone, including yourself, you are giving in to the false perception that you must have been weakened through attack. Being weakened is impossible, therefore forgiveness must be natural. It lifts the burdens from our spirit and allows us to move forward toward recognizing our perfection without the weight that goes along with a heavy heart. You will feel light and free because you no longer carry the burden of your illusions; you will release yourself and the one you thought imprisoned you at the same time. You will be free to let your truth soar and to "let your light shine."

~ **Exercises** ~

Are there any incidents involving your parents or primary caregivers that were very powerful and left you with a feeling of being unappreciated, hurt, humiliated, or unloved? Do you still cringe or get angry? Write down each incident in as much detail as you can.

Can you remember any incidents involving a teacher or mentor, that were very powerful and left you feeling unappreciated, hurt, humiliated, or unloved? Do you still cringe or get angry? Write down each incident in as much detail as you can.

Can you remember any incidents involving strangers or other children that were very powerful and left you feeling unappreciated, hurt, humiliated, or unloved? Do you still cringe or get angry? Write down each incident in as much detail as you can.

Can you think of any incidences that reinforce any of your childhood wounds as an adult, any situations that left you feeling unappreciated, hurt, humiliated, or unloved? Write down the incident in as much detail as you can.

Can you think of any incidents in your adult life that left you feeling helpless or forsaken? Write down each incident in as much detail as you can. Include any feelings you can express.

Write a letter to the people who hurt you in the past and explain to them how they hurt you. You don't have to send it, just putting it on paper should be enough. Many times, people have no idea what effect they have had on others. A passing comment may have an emotional impact for life. If you feel compelled, you can call the person and explain to him or her in an non-confrontational, loving way how the incident affected you. If you cannot communicate in a loving way, it is best to keep your thoughts between you and the paper.

Is there a common thread among the experiences you have written down? What are all of these experiences telling you that you need to let go of in order to experience yourself as free and whole?

~ Healing and the Mind ~

"And why do you look at the speck in your brother's eye, but do not perceive the plank in your own eye? Or how can you say to your brother, "Brother, let me remove the speck that is in your eye," when you yourself do not see the plank that is in your own eye? Hypocrite! First remove the plank from your own eye, and then you will see clearly to remove the speck that is in your brother's eye." - Luke 6:41-42

To fulfill my role in the Divine order and help others help themselves, I first had to heal myself. The instant I healed my mind of my false beliefs, evidence of the healing was reflected in my thoughts. I no longer obsessed over my body and weight. The release of these burdensome thoughts allowed me to finally release my weight problem, which I so strongly identified with, yet rejected at the same time. I am still very weight conscious, but I am much easier on myself and know that I can change my weight at any time. I now feel sexy regardless of my weight, and my experience reflects those thoughts.

Another result of my healing was that I no longer obsess over other women's bodies. I stopped seeing my perceived imperfections in them because I no longer saw such imperfections in myself. I no longer reinforced my feelings of inadequacy because I no longer had the false perception that I was inadequate.

My husband helped me to know myself as lovable. He has always been a great supporter and has always encouraged me to follow my heart, even during times when I thought it would be better for both of us if I just championed the status quo. Because of his support, I have always been encouraged to fulfill my higher purpose. In doing so, I have had the freedom of digging deeply into my soul and dredging up the pain of my past so that I can heal it. After I got married and had that first "moment of clarity" when I started jumping around the room and thanking all those people who inflicted the supposed pain upon me, Andy was not one of those people. Aside from my parents who never intentionally hurt me, Andy is the only one who had a strong impact on me who is still alive. It took me a long time to come to an understanding of what I had to gain from that experience, and the time it took was certainly worth the wait.

Although I was not clinically ill, I harbored emotional scars that I carried with me wherever I went. All healing first starts in the mind. Healing occurs through a release of a mindset or way of thinking that has manifested in our bodies.

In the 1940s my grandmother had tuberculosis. She was married to a minister, and they had a small boy named Wilburn, who was two years old. Back then, to treat tuberculosis, doctors quarantined you to a room and tracked the progress of the disease once a week using a machine that you breathed into. There was no cure; all you could do was pray and wait.

After being in the hospital for several months and yearning to hold her little boy, my grandmother decided one night to pray for healing. She said something like, "Dear Lord, I have tried to live according to your will, and I yearn so much to hold little Wilburn. Please, I will dedicate my life to serving you if only I can hold my baby again." After praying for a long while, a feeling of peace and love came over my grandmother, and she went to sleep knowing that she had been healed.

The next day was the day of her weekly test to track the progress of the tuberculosis. She knew going in that the Lord had healed her. The technician hooked her up to the machine as usual, and after several minutes, thought the machine was malfunctioning, because it could not detect any tuberculosis. She told my grandmother the machine was broken and they needed to hook her up to a different one. When the technician hooked my grandmother up to the next machine, the same thing happened. After several hours, ten more machines, and many more tests, the room was filled with doctors and technicians trying to figure out what was going on.

Finally, that night, my grandmother's doctor came in and said, "Mrs. Schram, we can find no more tuberculosis in your lungs. Tomorrow you will start your rehabilitation."

Some people may say that God healed my grandmother and they would be correct. Some people would say my grandmother healed herself, and they too would be correct. Some might say that her desire to hold her baby again is what healed my grandmother, and they would be correct. Some would say that something in her body chemistry triggered a remission, and they too would be correct.

Our divinity is housed in our minds. I believe in miracles and in spontaneous healing. All illness stems from somewhere in our minds. Once we release the debilitating thought of disease, our bodies spontaneously heal. Sometimes we need to experience suffering in order to activate our desire for change.

"Without suffering, there can be no progress" – Frederick Douglas. I saw this quotation painted on a building while leaving Manhattan one afternoon. I thought, "Wow, that's it!" We need to experience feelings of suffering, longing, failure, and the like in order to recognize that these are things we don't want. We also need to experience them on a level where we feel we have been beaten down and have nowhere to go but up. Frederick Douglas meant, that unless we experience these intense feelings of despair, sometimes we have no incentive to change the status quo.

I like to think of it as if we are all our own house and the universe is throwing rocks at our house to tell us it's time to take action. At first, we hear a light "tap, tap" of the smallest pebbles hitting our window. If we ignore the pebbles and refuse to listen to the message the universe will soon start throwing larger rocks and eventually break the window. The size and intensity of the rocks will increase until, finally, there will be a wrecking ball knocking down your house.

A friend and I were discussing the wrecking-ball experience that occurred in her family. Catherine grew up in a large Catholic family. Her father had always been a great provider for his family but was never overly affectionate. Last year, he went into a coma, and for the first time the family has been allowed to shower this man with the affection that he has always needed, yet was always too guarded to display. The universe forced him into a situation in which he was the one being cared for by his loved ones instead of always being the provider. My friend said that her father's being in a coma was one of the most amazing experiences her family has ever gone through, and her whole family has pulled together to nurture and love the man who has always given all and asked for nothing in return.

After her father had been in a coma for a year, the family made a decision to discontinue life support. The family nurses, doctors and everyone who had taken part in nurturing Catherine's father was present when they decided to shut off the machinery. There were many tears as well as a sense of relief. Everyone there had been the life-support system for a man.

Catherine's father was forced into a situation that caused him to be nurtured by those he loved during the last year of his life. Had he not gone into a coma, he would never have experienced his family's love for him. He also brought them together and through the experience, they all learned how to give back. The coma forced him to receive the gift of love.

Another wrecking-ball experience also happened in my family. In 1980, three weeks after finalization of my parents' divorce, my father married to a woman named Beverly. Previous to that, my aunt told my father that, were it not for her, my brother, sister, and I would be orphans, because my mother who had custody of us, was never around. As a result of my mother's absence, my aunt was left with the job of primary caregiver, which basically consisted of feeding us and giving us a place to live. My aunt could not handle the physical and emotional demands of five children, including her own, and I'm sure she felt very used. Her telling my father that we would be orphans was the catalyst he needed to marry and have us move in with him and his new wife.

My father is a person of great integrity and honor. He had been dating Beverly for a few months and knew that he wanted to marry her, but he wanted to set a good example for his kids and believed that one must teach by example. He also knew that Beverly would be the woman who raised us from that point on, and he wanted to do what he felt was the honorable thing: marry her and then invite his children to live with them as married parents. Beverly agreed.

In December 1979, we went to spend Christmas vacation with my father and Beverly, and they told us that from then on, we would be living with them. From that point on, the lives of my brother, sister, and I changed dramatically. We were part of a loving family who provided and cared for us, and we had all the love and attention we needed to grow up and be productive, self-confident people.

Although my father and Beverly had an amicable relationship with my mother, Beverly always held some deep-seated resentment toward my mother. The conclusions I draw are based on my scope of knowledge about Beverly's life and the pain and anger she carried in her body.

In 1983, after months of knowing she had a lump in her armpit, Beverly went to get it checked. The doctors found that she not only had breast cancer, but it had also infected 90 percent of the lymph nodes in her left arm. After very aggressive chemotherapy, her breast cancer went into remission.

At the time, Beverly was being a mother to my father's three children and was also a flight attendant for TWA. In 1986, after my siblings and I had lived with my father and Beverly for six years, my mother sued for retroactive child support, dating back to 1981. My mother claimed that she had primary custody, and my father was being delinquent on his child-support payments. My father and Beverly had paid for all of our needs, plus alimony and partial child-support payments, which my mother had agreed to six years earlier.

Shortly after my mother filed he lawsuit, Beverly experienced a cancer recurrence. The CAT scan showed tumors in her liver and spleen. This time, she was asked if she would like to be a participant in an experimental drug program. She had been through traditional chemotherapy and saw the new drug as hope. She believed in her doctors, and she believed that the experimental drug would free her from cancer. She believed her work was not finished, and she believed in God. After four months, the tumors disappeared and there were no traces of the cancer in her body.

Beverly came to visit me and my new fiancée in August 1997. We thought she looked great. During her visit she and I had a huge argument about her not wanting my biological mother to be at the wedding. A couple of months passed, and I had been scheduled for a four-day weekend in mid-October. As soon as I saw that long weekend on my calendar, my fiancée suggested that I go home to visit Beverly.

We bought tickets and my brother, who was also living in the Twin Cities, decided to join us. My father had been telling us that Beverly was doing well. I believe now he had been living in denial; perhaps she appeared to him to be doing well because he saw her every day, and the decay was gradual enough for him to overlook, but we were not prepared for what we saw.

When we arrived at my father's house, we saw, a Beverly who had aged forty years in the past two months. In August, she had been a lively, spirited being who was in love with her son-in-law to be and was concerning herself with wedding details. She was now unable to keep down the simplest of foods and didn't look like she would live another week. She needed help getting off the couch and had to eat all of her meals in liquid form. We had been planning to get married in April, but after seeing her, we decided that we would get married over Thanksgiving, hoping that she would live to see the wedding day.

As a result of my father's denial, my sister had no idea of Beverly's condition. I called my sister and told her that if she ever wanted to see Bev alive again, she had better get there fast. My sister went to visit the next weekend, stayed with her a week, and Beverly died October 30.

Over the years, Beverly had been carrying around a lot of pain and anger. The anger manifested itself in the form of breast cancer. It attacked her femininity and took away her breast, an organ meant to feed babies and that men love. I believe she saw my mother as a nemesis and the cause of her cancer.

Before we had that last visit with Beverly, I had contacted a spiritual healer on her behalf. The healer told me that he had a 98 percent cure rate with women with breast cancer. There is a lesson here: never use the ego to brag about a gift that God bestows. Beverly decided to go see the spiritual healer, and although she did not live long after seeing him, I do believe he helped her.

After seeing the healer, Beverly seemed calmer. She recounted to me that he had her close her eyes and visualize looking in the mirror. She had to tell him who was the person renting space in her body. She saw the face of my mother in the mirror. He instructed her to tell my mother to leave, and Beverly did as she was told. After the healing, Beverly finally let go of the anger she had been harboring toward my mother.

The lesson she needed to learn was forgiveness. She had been given several opportunities to learn it. Each time the disease came back, it coincided with a period when she was angry with my mother.

Once Beverly learned to forgive, she moved on to a place where there is no pain, where she was freed of her bodily limitations. Beverly's work was done. She came into our family to be our mother, a role she always defended. To this day, I am grateful that she came into my life and raised me as her daughter.

~ Exercises ~

If you have any health problems, can you identify the portion of your thinking that has manifested itself in your body? For example, if you have breast cancer, is there something in your belief system that leads you to question your own femininity? If you have diabetes, do you crave more sweetness in your life?

What toxic beliefs might you be carrying around that have contributed to your illness?

~ To Have All Give All ~

"Judge not, and you shall not be judged. Condemn not, and you shall not be condemned. Forgive, and you will be forgiven. Give, and it will be given to you: good measure, pressed down, shaken together, and running over will be put in your bosom. For with the same measure that you use, it will be measured back to you" - *Luke 6:37-40*

The Bible quotation at the beginning of this chapter addresses the universal law, what we give, we receive. We treat others the way we would treat ourselves. We can be abusive toward others or we can be kind. The choice is always ours to make. Whatever you would give another, you must also desire for yourself. Whatever you give the universe returns to you multiplied. The law works both for things we want and things we don't want in our lives.

Whatever we extend to others increases in us. For example, all of my speeches are about various aspects of my personal development. My pattern for writing and delivering speeches has been as follows: As I gain understanding about certain aspects of my development, I write a speech that discusses what I have learned.

I noticed that, after each speech, I gained a more solid understanding of what I had just imparted to my audience. As I understood these concepts on a more intimate level, I would then gain more insight, which would further increase my understanding of myself, God, my fellow humans, and the universe. Many of us believe that these are all the same entity, so it makes sense that I have gained a better understanding of all these aspects.

I have been imparting knowledge and wisdom to my fellow Toastmasters, who have grown and benefited from my teachings. The "reward" has been that I have gained more knowledge and insight to share.

A Course in Miracles states: "To have all, give all." This idea corresponds perfectly with my experience. I have given wisdom, knowledge, and insight, so I have gained more insight, wisdom, and knowledge. Everything we experience is a form of energy, and this formula is true for everything.

Be that which you desire. If you desire more love, give love. If you desire more money, give money. If you desire more happiness, give happiness. How do you do this? There is probably a nursing home or hospital nearby where people are lonely and in desperate want of visitors. If you desire love and companionship, be the love and companionship those folks need. Perhaps you are in want of a house; there are organizations that help people build and buy houses. Volunteer with Habitat for Humanity or other service organizations that help people with housing. If you want more money, use what financial resources you have to help others who have less than you. You can help raise money through a walk-a-thon or other types of fundraisers that help people collect money for helping others. The list goes on and on. Whatever we give expands in us, so whatever you desire, fill that desire for someone else.

I wanted greater opportunities to speak in public. I decided to create a speakers bureau for Toastmasters in the Washington, D.C., region. I found that each time I booked a speaking engagement for one of my speakers, someone contacted me to do a speaking engagement outside of the bureau. In other words, what goes around comes around. The more I gave of myself in obtaining speaking engagements for others, the more I received in the form of speaking engagements.

We can give only what we have. Give pain and you increase it in yourself. Give love, and you increase that. The people who tried to impose their pain upon me were increasing it in themselves. Because they had the pain to give in the first place, they were only increasing it in themselves, not giving it away. It works both ways. If I want to give someone a flower, yet I do not have a flower, I do not have it to give. If I want to give someone love, but all I have is pain and feelings of isolation, pain and isolation is what I have to give. If I try to give away my pain and isolation to others in an attempt to get rid of those feelings, I only increase them feelings in myself.

Had my tormentors not harbored a great deal of pain, they would not have had the pain to give to me. Because they were also suffering from the same pain they were trying to give me, they already claimed it for themselves, and by trying to give it away, they increased it in themselves as well.

When we judge, condemn, criticize, or attack another, we must ask ourselves what it says about us if we feel the need to attack that person. I found that my perceived flaws were disguised in my judgments of others. Because I disliked my body and tried hard to dissociate from my body, I subconsciously judged other women according to their bodies. My judgment of others increased my self-judgment.

If I saw a woman who was more slender than I, I would think, "Wow! She looks great in those jeans," or "She doesn't look like she's had three kids," or "Yup, she can probably eat that ice-cream cone; I'm sure she has a really fast metabolism." If the woman was heavier, I ripped her apart in my mind. My thoughts were more like, "Why is she wearing spandex? She has at least sixty pounds to lose," or "She shouldn't be eating ice cream; she belongs on a treadmill," or "That's a nice suit, but it still doesn't hide her fat."

With the women who were more slender than I, I was reinforcing my own feelings of inadequacy in comparison with them and placing them on a pedestal that I thought was unreachable. I felt inadequate compared to slender women and reinforced my own low opinion of myself. I was not complimenting slender women, I was denigrating myself.

The women who were heavier than I were reflecting back all the characteristics I desperately wanted to dissociate from myself. I had emotional stock in being fat and hating my body, so that's what I noticed in other women. Heavier women mirrored back everything I didn't want to recognize in myself, and I reinforced that those qualities were unacceptable. If I had had no personal emotional investment in that trait, I would not have been harsh and critical.

All the experiences that stick out in my mind revealed many similarities between me and the people who were judging or criticizing me. In the experience:

- My tormentors were seeing me reflected in themselves.
- They were trying to give away a part of themselves that they had rejected.
- They identified the trait in me that they had rejected in themselves and told me it was offensive.
- They were reinforcing their own feelings of inadequacy by pointing them out in me.
- They were all suffering from the same pain they were inflicting on me

We've all heard the expression "It takes one to know one." When we judge another we must then point the finger at ourselves to find out what the person is showing us about ourselves. We do not notice things about others that we do not associate with ourselves. All of these people identified in me something that they identified in themselves. If they didn't feel that they possessed the same quality, they would not have noticed it in me.

The universal law works with everything we give away. A friend of mine recently packed up everything she had and moved down South to be near her ailing parents. She moved on blind faith, with her son and two dogs in her little pop-up camper, and no job prospects lined up. She needed some cash but didn't want to ask anyone because she felt it would create an obligation. I told her I would send her a check and that I didn't care what she did with it, that it was a gift. I asked her to please not feel obligated to tell me what she did with it and it was hers to do with as she pleased.

Three days after she received the check, I received an e-mail from a woman I met at a conference telling me that a speaker she had lined up for a women's retreat had had a heart attack and they needed to fill the speaking slot. The planned workshop was to be eight hours long and she was looking for someone who could provide an eight-hour program for the retreat. She asked if I was interested in filling the slot. I was free that weekend, so I told her I could do it.

The speaking engagement paid well over four times the amount I had given my friend. The request came out of the blue, and I can't help but think that the reason I was contacted for that engagement was because I had given money to someone else when she needed it. The speaking opportunity was the universe returning to me manyfold what I had given away.

Don't be afraid to give of yourself. Whatever you give another, you increase for yourself. Everything you have is given to you by the universe, and it is up to you to either allow the flow of the universe to move through you or to stop with you. To be abundant and prosperous in all areas of life, you must be free to give all that you have with love and gratitude for what you have, and trust that the universe will reward your generosity.

~ Exercises ~

What do you desire to increase in your life? Do you see a block in your ability to give what you desire? If so, describe in as much detail as possible what you desire and how you can be that for others.

Reflect on your own experiences and describe a few examples that illustrate how this principle has presented itself in your life. Have you found that the more you gave of a certain aspect of yourself, the more you drew that very thing to yourself?

What have you given, and how has that thing increased in your life as a result of your giving?

If you have not given of yourself, do you notice a lack of flow in any areas of your life?

~ **Just Ask the Universe** ~

"Men give advice; God gives guidance."
- Leonard Ravenhill

It helps to ask the universe to help you out when you do not see a favorable outcome. I've noticed that if I just let go of my expectations and attachments to what the outcome should be, things work out better than I could have planned.

I was scheduled to do a presentation for a local TV program last August. The dress rehearsal was in July, and I was scheduled to go on in July only if someone dropped out and the program director needed me to fill in. In the meantime, my cousin, a navy pilot, had just come back from Operation Iraqi Freedom and was going to be visiting my father in upstate New York the same day I was scheduled to record the TV program in August. I knew I had to do the television program, yet I wanted to see my cousin. I started getting a little stressed about not being able to see him, then decided I would let go of the outcome and things would work out as they should. I figured that there was a reason I was tentatively scheduled for two dates and I would let the universe take care of the details.

As it turned out, I was wise in handing the outcome over to the universe. I had my dress rehearsal in July and the program director told me that one person had not gotten back to her yet, and I might be taking the other guest's place. I received confirmation the following week that I would be appearing in July instead of August. This worked out perfectly because I was able to see my cousin and get the TV appearance out of the way before leaving for vacation.

I have also heard that once you are on the right track, the universe will send you opportunities that relate to your purpose. At one Toastmasters meeting, I was talking to a friend who said, "If you truly want to be a motivational speaker, what you need to do is write a book and spread your message by going on a book tour." Intuitively, I knew this was true and I replied, "You're right, Jim, but I don't even know how to get started."

A few minutes later, a funny thing happened. There was a woman named Kayt who was interested in knowing a little bit more about me because she liked the speech I had presented. I told her that I had had an awakening of spirit a few years prior and it all came to me in a "spiritual revelation, corny as that may sound." She asked if I had considered recording my message in a book, and I told her that my friend, Jim, had just said the same thing, but, I didn't know how to write a book.

She said, "You start with one chapter at a time." This plan made sense, and that afternoon I went home and started writing. When I got stuck, it just so happened that my husband was reading Steven King's autobiography, in which he describes the book-writing process. He instructs readers to write down everything they can think of and worry about the details of organizing it later. I needed that nudge when I felt stuck.

After a while, I put the question out there, "Okay, universe, I'm getting my book under way but I'm going to need a good editor." Two weeks later, I was a guest speaker at another club, where I met a woman named Fran. After talking with Fran for a few minutes, she told me that she edits for music textbooks that are used in schools. I asked her how I could go about finding an editor for my type of book, and she told me that the main difference between editors is their experience level and that her business was built on the foundation that she can edit anything written in the English language. I found my editor right there.

A little later, I posed the question, "Okay, now that I have my editor, how do I go about finding a publisher?" I had been told that getting published was the most difficult challenge of all. Again, a couple of weeks later, I took a book off my bookshelf that I had been meaning to read for several years, but had never gotten around to it. Inside the book, used as a bookmark, was it of an old friend I had lost touch with years ago. On the business card was the information I needed to get in contact my friend, Joshuah, who had started a publishing company around the same time I was dating him. I had been thinking about Joshuah on and off for years and even tried to contact him several times, but because he has such a common name I didn't know where to start looking. The company name on the card was unique, so it took very little time to locate him and tell him that I had started my first book.

I have found that just putting my desire out into the universe and allowing it to handle the details is a great way of drawing what I need to help me accomplish my goals. In addition to asking the universe to do certain things for me, like leading me to an editor and publisher, it has also been sending me more and more speaking engagements with very little effort on my part. If you tell the universe or your guides what you desire, and ask for help in moving things along, you can let go of the outcome and the universe tends to work things out in your favor, even if you don't recognize at first that it is in your favor. Time will show you how well things worked out.

I have also started keeping a spirit journal, in which I delegate authority to the universe by indicating tasks with three stars before and after a request. *** Please help me with this particular problem... ***

I have noticed that my requests are being addressed with incredible speed. Because I have written them down, I can go back and see what I have delegated to the universe and can see where the universe is working with me toward my goals. Delegating authority and seeing results gives me more confidence that I am not alone and have help all the time. All I need to do is ask and assistance will flow.

~ **Exercises** ~

Life Manifestation

A life manifestation is a tool you can use to tell the universe what you desire. Write your life manifestation in the positive and the present. For example, in my life manifestation, I have things like "I am a feminine, sexy woman. I am a highly successful motivational speaker and reach millions of people with my message of love."

Include anything and everything in your life manifestation that you would like to draw into your life. Read it out loud to yourself in the mirror a few times a month. The energy of your words and hearing your manifestation in the spoken word will guide you to the experiences of reaching your goals. Eventually, you will notice that things will start falling into place and your life will be almost effortless, because you have indicated to the universe what you desire, and the universe will place your desires right on your doorstep.

~ Giving Away Our Power ~

"I'm black, I don't feel burdened by it and I don't think it's a huge responsibility. It's part of who I am. It does not define me." - Oprah Winfrey

When we define ourselves, we are limiting ourselves. There is no freedom in labeling oneself, no matter how glamorous the label might appear. The only self-definition I can think of that would not be limiting in any way would be to say, "I am infinite and limitless."

The fact that we label and define ourselves indicates that we feel we are separate and different from other people. We set boundaries to our own experience and therefore limit ourselves through the definitions we set. Through our feelings of separation we can understand the qualities we use to limit ourselves, and we can see how we choose to view ourselves.

After my second daughter was born, I decided to lose all the extra weight I had been carrying around my whole life. I joined a weight-loss program and went from a size eighteen to a size eight in two years. I had consciously decided that

I no longer wanted to define myself as "fat." Additionally, I had reached a place in my development where I recognized that I did not have to accept the definition I perceived that others had placed upon me. I saw that through my belief in my limitation of being overweight, I was limiting myself, not only physically but also emotionally.

Because of my definition of self, I was very overweight. I identified myself with being overweight and my body complied with what I told it that it was. I completely identified with my body and wanted nothing more than to be thin; however, according to the messages I was giving my body, I was fat. I chose to define myself as fat, and I chose to not like that definition; therefore, I was imposing a definition upon myself and rejecting myself because of the definition I imposed upon myself simultaneously.

How do you judge others? Once you identify the things you judge in others, you will see traits you have rejected in yourself. Over the next week, pay attention to your judgments. You will learn a great deal about what you are unwilling to see in yourself. Your observations will direct you to what you need to accept and love in yourself.

Although I'm much smaller than I was, I still sometimes have a hard time seeing myself realistically. I have carried around that "fat" limitation for so long that I will be working on healing my self-image for a long time. Healing my self-image is part of my growth process. We teach what we most need to learn. The more I teach others how to free themselves of their own limitations, the more I tell myself that the essence of my teachings is my truth, not the poor self-image I carried for so many years.

I have made great strides in healing my self-image. A good way to determine how we define ourselves is to pay attention to our observations of others. It has been said that the world is our mirror, and recognizing ourselves in others is the key to understanding how we perceive ourselves. I no longer judge women according to their bodies. Instead I look on them with quiet observation and have a more compassionate approach. For example, I work out three times a week for ninety minutes. I take two classes back to back: one is high-intensity cross-training and the other is a body-sculpting class.

The combination is very intense, and I have grown to love it. Previously, I had been swimming laps for an hour three days a week, and a few months ago, switched to the ninety-minute workout. At first, I hated it. I was sore all the time and didn't think I could last. Three months after starting the class, I looked forward to the intensity of it. We work our muscles in different ways, so I always come home with new aches, ranging from feeling it when I am going up the stairs to working my abdominals so much that it hurts to cough. I love having these aches because I know I'm doing something good for myself. I have friends who are going through the same thing. Everyone else in the class feels sore too, and we are all in it together, sweating and groaning, because we are all being pushed to our limits.

A new woman recently joined the class. She is obviously dedicated to becoming healthier because she had lost seventy pounds and had another hundred to go. She made it to her second class, and showing up is half the battle, especially after attending the first class, where every muscle is sore for the next week. During a portion of the workout, we are always told to pick a partner to do some of the exercise intervals. I asked her if she would like to be my partner, and she agreed.

I know I have healed a great deal in my self-perception, because of the mere act of asking this woman to be my partner. Previously, I would not have asked someone who was a hundred pounds overweight to be my partner because I would have prejudged her before ever getting to the point of finding out her name. I would have seen my reflection in her and internally attacked both of us because she would have been showing me all of my own perceived deficiencies. I would have avoided her because my self perception was so negative that I would have been seething with contempt, which I would have thought was directed toward her but would really have been directed towards myself.

I viewed my workout partner as more of a sister in the weight-loss struggle; I asked her out of the compassion of having been there and knowing what an enormous step it is to dedicate oneself to this type of workout regiment. I saw her as a woman with some of the same issues as me. By having her as my workout partner, I could give her encouragement to make it through the workout, let her know that others in the class have been there, and maybe make a friend while I was at it. I saw her as a person struggling with her body and trying to get to a point of self-acceptance, a woman with issues similar to my own, who thinks and feels, instead of seeing her merely as her exterior shell.

During my teens and twenties, it didn't matter whether women were slender or overweight; I judged everyone and saw what I thought I was or was not in each judgmental thought. I was so desperately trying to dissociate my body from myself that the thought of even stepping into a gym or aerobics class was a major turn-off. I would rather work out by myself by walking or swimming than feel I was being judged by others in an aerobics class.

The truth is that I couldn't handle my own judgmental thoughts, but because I projected that thought, I interpreted that others would be judging me. I am the projector and my world is the big silver screen. I would have placed upon a pedestal a more slender woman by seeing her as physically superior to me, and I would have thought she was judging me because of my body. What seemed like a compliment or a "positive judgment" on my part was a clever way to belittle myself and reinforce my own feelings of inadequacy. A heavier woman would have been directly mirroring back to me the exact trait that I wanted to dissociate from myself. By judging her, I was reinforcing my own feelings of inadequacy by pinpointing the same "flaw" in her.

I carried the feelings of physical inadequacy with me into adulthood. Only in the last few years have I understood why I had to experience them. I thought all along that I was separate from others through my "defective" body. As a result, the foundation for my greatest strength was the experience of knowing what it was like to feel unlovable, when the love I was so desperately searching for was actually within me. I needed to merely identify, acknowledge, and understand that I had been wrong about myself all along. I needed to see where I thought I was lacking something in order to understand that there was never any lack. All my lack and limitations dwell within my own mind.

We have forgotten that we are divine beings and have

perceived ourselves as being flawed. The correction of our false perception is what will free us to know our perfection. We all have a special gift hidden in the form of our perceived flaws. All of us have a special way in which we feel we are separate and different from the rest of humanity. This perceived flaw is where the gift lies, perfectly disguised, waiting for our recognition of truth.

My special gift was disguised as my feelings of physical inadequacy and lack of self-worth. I am not the only person on the planet who has felt physically inadequate; however, my feelings of lack combined with my own likes, dislikes, and experiences are what make me unique. Once I realized that I was as perfect now as I was at my inception, before I had a body, I realized that my life had been a giant illusion that I had created.

My illusion was that I identified with my outer world and things that I thought separated me from others. By comparing myself to the world I saw, I perceived I was imperfect. I was identifying with my vanity and my ego, which I alone created. I was neither flawed nor worthless; I only perceived myself as imperfect because I didn't recognize that the flaw was in my own thinking.

Once I understood my thoughts as the creative force behind my experience, I realized that my body has always given me exactly what I have focused on. I understood that my negative thoughts about my body have created a body that I did not like, and that my body has been a perfect and natural extension of my divinity, my divinity being the thoughts that I use to create how I perceive myself and my world. Our divinity is the creative force behind how we perceive ourselves.

Our consciousness is an extension of God's mind, and we are constantly creating ourselves anew. God has no opinion about our physical or emotional limitations because limitation is not of God's creation. Our experiences of lack are our own creations, and we have the power to express our divinity and limitlessness through the way we respond to our experiences. Whatever thoughts we have about ourselves or our world will be reflected in our experience and will be validated through our divine creative processes.

Affirmations are tools we can use to reprogram our thinking. Similar to life manifestations, affirmations are short belief statements we tell ourselves to change the way we experience the world. For affirmations to work, they must be written in the positive form. "I am a thin person," instead of "I am no longer a fat person." The second affirmation focuses on what I do not want, which means I would bring into my life what I did not want if I used it as a affirmation.

Affirmations must be written in the present, because tomorrow never comes. Say, "I am a thin person" instead of "I will be a thin person." Say your affirmations to yourself constantly hundreds of times a day for six weeks and you will notice a radical change in the way you experience the world.

~ Exercises ~

How has your self-definition limited you? Can you see how by defining yourself you have limited your experience and access to your personal power? Describe in as much detail as possible how your thoughts have limited you and steps you can take toward releasing yourself from those limiting bonds.

How have you drawn exactly what you have been focusing on into your life?

If you could be anything or do anything without limitations, what would you do or be? Write it into an affirmation. You might write, "I am an award-winning author" or, I sell more houses than any agent in my real estate company this year," or "I get my master's in adult education." Write down your affirmation and tape it to your bedroom or bathroom mirror. Say it hundreds of times a day. In six weeks, note how your life has begun to bring you whatever you desire.

~ Claiming Our Power ~

"The specialness he chose to hurt himself did God appoint to be the means for his salvation, from the very instant the choice was made. His special sin was made his special grace. His special hate became his special love."

— *A Course in Miracles*

No human who ever lived, including all of the great masters, has had a greater part in bringing harmony to the universe than each of us has individually. Each of the great masters has fully understood that we are all equally divine and has taught this message in his or her own way. We are all great masters; we are all equally powerful; we are all one with God. We merely need to rid ourselves of the blocks that keep us from recognizing our own power. God is in each of us and it is up to us to recognize our divinity and accept ourselves as complete and whole. We must claim our power and take responsibility for correcting our false perceptions. By healing our own minds, we bring peace and harmony to the rest of humanity through our example.

We claim our power by accepting ourselves and ridding ourselves of negative and false notions that we are anything less than perfect. You were born to express and experience yourself fully, as the divine, perfect being you are. You do not claim your divinity by living up to the expectations of another, you claim it by accepting yourself as you are. You must be true to yourself, live according to who you are and who you wish to be, and trust in your inner greatness.

To remove the veils that obscure our truth, we must identify the traits we have rejected and replaced with our borrowed idea of what we think perfection should be like. We can do this by making a list of our least favorite attributes.

Once we have identified these characteristics, we can look into our past and find incidents where someone viewed that particular trait or as unacceptable or imperfect. The underlying trait becomes a nucleus for negative feelings. When stripped away and seen as just a trait, the otherwise offensive characteristic is viewed as benign, neither good nor bad. By embracing formerly rejected traits, we can then see that we are perfect and complete, and it's impossible to improve upon perfection. Only our limiting beliefs and our beliefs in imperfection cause us to experience ourselves as imperfect. Remove the imperfect thought and all that remains is perfection itself.

I came across an article written by Jon Snodgrass, Ph.D., which explained the concept of Your Special Function, according to A Course in Miracles. Your Special Function is another way of saying, your purpose. Here is the excerpt from the article:

"Your Special Function is the polar opposite of what you

believe to be the reality of your own guilt, sin, and victimization. Whatever you think is your problem, is your answer, what is missing is your gift, your weakness is your strength, your damnation is your salvation, your special dysfunction is your Special Function."

After reading this statement, I thought for a moment, "Okay, what's my special dysfunction? Well, I'm fat... No, I don't like myself... No, I don't love myself. What's the polar opposite of that?" This is the part where I was hit with a lightning bolt and thought, "My Special Function is to learn how to love myself and teach others how to love themselves!"

After that revelation, I experienced the most blissful state I have ever known. My gift came in the form of seeing the polar opposite of who I thought I was as my true self. That perfect perception came in the form of seeing myself as the opposite of my chosen incorrect perception. Through the understanding that my imperfections were merely a mistake in my self-perception, I freed my mind of the burden that kept me from experiencing myself as complete and whole. I knew what it was like to wallow in the depths of self-hatred, so it was only natural that, after healing that portion of my thinking, I would be the best person to help others to know how to love themselves and accept themselves as complete and whole.

The same dynamic occurs with recovering alcoholics. Only one who has been in the painful depths of alcoholism can understand the struggle of being an alcoholic and is therefore the best person for another alcoholic to lean on to remain sober. The reason why Alcoholics Anonymous members have sponsors is because the sponsors have benefited from the program. The sponsor has been there, has had a drinking problem, has overcome it, and knows what it is like. The sponsor is the person the recovering alcoholic leans on during difficult times. Additionally, the more the sponsor counsels the recovering alcoholic, the more likely the sponsor will remain sober. We teach what we most need to learn, and by teaching, we solidify our own teachings in our own minds.

Our experience differentiates us from our human companions and establishes our unique talents and strengths. Our beliefs about who we are determine how we can best use our strengths and talents. The combination of our likes, dislikes, experiences, strengths, loves, and beliefs paints the complete picture of how we can best use our gifts and do our best work. Because our experience is our unique gift, we already have everything we need to fulfill our highest human potential. But how do we figure out what that is?

We need to first figure out what we would like to do more than anything else. Look at your likes and dislikes, experiences, talents, and dreams, and bring into your awareness what you would truly like to do with your life. I know what my greatest gift to humanity is: it is releasing my limitations and showing others how to do the same through my example. I love to explore the nature of my mind and am constantly striving to free myself from my limitations.

I love to organize my ideas so that I can express them to others in any way that can to help people understand the dynamics of their own relationships. I love to help people understand why we act and react the way we do and empower them to take control of their destiny. I know that helping people free themselves of their limitations is my gift because it helps me to release mine. This is not to say that I no longer have limitations; however, the more limiting beliefs I release, the more love and freedom I experience in my life. I also love people and experiencing the love that I am. I express my loving nature through my interactions, and the more people I can touch, the happier I am.

The more limitations I release, the more power I allow myself, and the more creativity and spontaneity I allow myself to experience. Each time I release a tiny bit more, I have lifted another layer of a multilayered veil and can see more clearly what I was sent here to do. I had grown so accustomed to my own limiting thoughts or veils that obscured my vision that after a while I didn't even realize they were there. There are still many layers, yet with each unveiling, I am able to see my path more clearly. Lifting the veils is the key to understanding what my greatest gifts to humanity are. As each veil that obscures my light is lifted, I feel more free and loving of myself, I literally become my own best friend.

When we accept and love ourselves, we forgive ourselves and others who have seen us through false perceptions. When we change our minds, we change the way we experience our world. We recognize that had we not been misjudged, we would not have the opportunity to identify the limitations we believed to be true. Without the false perceptions of others, we would not be able to identify, correct, and heal our limiting beliefs.

We also do not need to strive to be anyone or do anything. We each embody the perfect qualities to successfully fulfill our unique role in the healing of our collective wounded spirit. When we claim our power as ours and stop giving it away to the ideas of who we think we should be, we cease the pain cycle, embrace who we are for ourselves, and become accepting of who we are. We love the God of our being with all our hearts.

Our power comes from the truth of our hearts. When we allow ourselves to be swayed by the opinions or judgments of others rather than following our own internal guidance, we give our power away. When we rely on the council of others rather than our own, we are telling ourselves we do not trust ourselves. Ignoring our truth reinforces the misperception that our thoughts are not good enough and someone else must be more trustworthy than we. When we claim our truth as our own and allow ourselves to be guided by our still small voice within, then we are showing ourselves that we love ourselves and we will be guided to our greatness through our own internal council.

~ Exercises ~

What negative ideas about yourself are you carrying around? Repeat the following phrase aloud in front of a mirror: "I love myself, body, mind, and spirit, completely and unconditionally." Write down any reaction you have. For example, if it makes you feel uncomfortable or silly saying it, write down why you think you feel this way.

How did you do in that last exercise? If you could look yourself in the eye, were being completely honest with yourself, had no problem saying that phrase to yourself and believed it down to the core, good. You are already well on your way. If you had a hard time saying it to yourself, even better.

Explore why you had a hard time. Search your feelings and write down in detail any negativity that comes out. Are there any people who are attached to these negative feelings? If so, write down who told you these things about yourself so you can identify who pointed out the "flaw" in you. Write in detail the people who said you had these flaws.

Can you see where you claimed ownership of someone else's judgment or opinion of you? Are there any common threads that you notice in the feelings you had?

~ **Your Part in the Whole** ~

"Each of us has a spark of life inside us, and our highest endeavor ought to be to set off that spark in one another."
- Kenny Ausubel

Whatever the reason you have chosen to incarnate, you have a very important part to fulfill. Sure, we will face struggles and challenges, but those are how we grow. If you fear the judgment of others and value the opinions of others more than your own counsel, you will never set yourself free from thoughts of condemnation.

I now understand exactly how powerful my mind is and that my thoughts create all of my experiences. After the speech competition, I wrote a life manifestation in which I wrote everything I wanted to be and to have happen in my life. My affirmation helps me focus on what I want instead of what I don't want.

When trying to make a decision relating to yourself, your future, your circumstances, remember: you are the best person to consult about your own path. Most people have had an idea about something then asked for a second opinion. If the person we ask voices his or her opinion and it contradicts our own, we may go with the other opinion. The best thing to do is always rely on your own inner voice, even if the outcome is not what you would have hoped. By trusting your intuition, you validate yourself and take responsibility for your life. If the person whose opinion you asked for then pressures you into doing things the way he or she wants, you will often feel that you have made the wrong decision.

Going against our inner guidance in deference to others is a way of dis-empowering ourselves. We then blame the other person for our mistake or allow him or her to make us feel bad for not following their advice. These are both ways of giving away our power.

Once we claim responsibility and ownership of our lives, we may feel that we made a wrong decision, but it is our decision and our mistake, not someone else's that led to an unfavorable outcome. Taking responsibility and ownership over our decisions is in itself empowering. If we choose to live according to the dictates of another because we wish to avoid conflict, we are squandering our power and cheating everyone else in the process. Claiming your power is the key to your fulfillment.

Every relationship and encounter we have is an opportunity to either be ourselves and embrace ourselves or to sell out and be who we think someone wants us to be. As we interact with each other, we are teaching lessons and affirming our beliefs about ourselves. The more encounters we have, the more we either compromise our truth or to validate our worth by remaining steadfastly true to ourselves. The more you act in accordance with the dictates of your own heart, the more you will have experiences that validate your reason for being. Do not let fear stop you from accomplishing your purpose. Fear is an illusion to keep you from having a fulfilling and enriching life. Banish the fear and limitation and let love be your guide.

In our search for love, we tend to mold ourselves to conform to who we think others would like us to be. We seek love but what we don't recognize is that we seek our own self-love. Self-love is complete self-acceptance. When we conform to who we think others would like us to be, we dim our brilliance and keep ourselves from experiencing our freedom to be our own unique expression of divinity.

Self-consciousness causes us to think we must be someone other than who we are to be accepted by others. When we become self-conscious, we start thinking and behaving according to how we think others want us to be. My friend, Ivan, shared his story of self-realization with me to illustrate how self-consciousness affects our ideas of who we think we are and how we reject ourselves in deference to how we think we should be.

"As I recall my childhood it was very pleasant and I felt special. In my teens my search for an identity outside the family gave me a reason for wrapping up and burying my true self for many years.

I started waking up in the beginning of January 2000 - I was thirty-four at the time and it might very well be the midlife crisis everybody talks of. My feelings for my wife had disappeared and I wanted to be anywhere but with her. My son was not enough to keep me in the marriage. So I left.

I started a self-realization process in which I changed my looks, my appearances and my mood. I used to be a "serious" person that was only interested in facts and what could be measured. Religion and the spiritual world was treated with contempt by me ever since I renounced the religion of my parents around the age of 14 due to the inconsistency I found in scriptures and morality.

I started becoming a smiling, casual and honest guy. I felt I was growing very quickly spiritually. I read dozens of books, took up meditating and philosophy studies as well as reading about all major and minor religions. I started seeing the similarities between the religions more than the differences. My horizons broadened.

I started to hear people comment on my change, and congratulating me for the improvement. At first I was very proud of the comments. I liked to be popular. Later I started wondering about the need for approval, and decided to be true to my self no matter what, a promise that I still try to keep.

All along I had tried to figure out and analyze things, rather than feel things. Recently I have become increasingly aware that feeling is also a way of understanding. I now use my feelings to understand my process of awakening.

My understanding continues to expand and I have begun to feel very fortunate that there are so many things to learn and so many things to teach. All aspects of life are worth a close study. I have now realized that it's possible to access all information inside oneself.

My visions for the future include a better world for our children, which means they and we should be taught to be accepting, understanding, listening, smiling, forgiving, loving humans. Moreover I have a vision concerning relationships of all kinds. I have a strong feeling that our energy levels need to be heightened and remain high in order for us to grow as spiritual beings. One way is to stay focused on living now. Another way is to get together and live in Conscious Communities. They are already popping up around the globe. Whatever the reason for wanting such a community, it can only be a step forward, since the present form of living doesn't seem to be working given that we say we want peace but peace is far from a reality.

My growth will continue and I feel very grateful knowing that now is the only time there is—forever. Love is the way of being—for all. Giving is the way of creating who I am in the highest version of me."

Ivan has been living according to his truth for about seven years. He has recently decided to quit his job as the head of broadcast for a television network and to follow his calling of liberating his spirit through laughter yoga.

He had become a serious teenager by conforming to who he thought others wanted him to be. Now that he is reclaiming himself and living according to his truth, he is finding delight and fulfillment by following his path. In addition to the laughter yoga, he is holding a vision for a future social paradigm in which we live cooperatively with each other and teach acceptance of ourselves and our children through conscious community. This is Ivan's dream for himself and as he embraces himself, the impact he has on the consciousness of the rest of us is elevated.

The complete acceptance of yourself is what leads to self-realization. You must abandon all forms of outside validation and live according to your truth and only your truth. Honoring your truth and trusting in yourself leads to self-realization and enlightenment. By being true to yourself you will find fulfillment, love, and enlightenment. Through your self-realization you will be liberated from the bonds of social and cultural oppression and find freedom in being you. When you no longer conform to who you think you should be, you will find that you live life consciously, brilliantly and fully.

You already have all the tools you need to fulfill your unique highest contribution to humanity, which is also your highest contribution to yourself. Your purpose is found through correcting false perceptions and living the truth of your being. Once you begin to embrace yourself consciously, your higher purpose becomes glaringly clear.

Ivan reinvented himself by releasing his social, religious, and moral bonds. He released the things he felt he must conform to in order to be accepted. Once he started accepting himself fully, he started living the life of his dreams. By being his highest idea of who he is, he affects those around him by living fully and with purpose. By living his highest idea of his truth, he illuminates through his example the path for others to find their way.

~ Exercises ~

When figuring out your highest contribution to humanity, it helps to make a list. Make the list all inclusive and be as honest with yourself as possible. Include three columns:

1. Positive traits, traits that hold a positive meaning for you.
2. Neutral traits, traits you have that hold no positive or negative meaning for you.
3. Negative traits, traits that hold negative meaning for you.

In each column, name as many traits as you can. Include as many physical, emotional, mental, and spiritual traits as you can. Don't be afraid if some of the things you list seem to contradict other things, just write. I, for example, can be both aggressive and passive, depending upon the situation. Be thorough and honest with yourself. If you have traits you would rather not mention, mention them anyway. They are an important part of who you are.

Look at the traits that seem contradictory. Can you identify what triggers you to respond in this way? For example, I am generally patient with my kids unless I feel pressed for time and they are not cooperating with me. If I feel pressed, I become short tempered and irritable. My internal pressure is my trigger or the fear that I will not accomplish my task on time and I attribute to my kids lack of cooperation with me.

Once you've made your lists of traits, ask yourself what is important to you. What do you enjoy most, and what makes you happiest? When you figure it out, take steps in the direction of your happiness and you will find that with each baby step, you will feel like it is a giant leap toward greater fulfillment.

~ **On Purpose** ~

"Neither a lofty degree of intelligence nor imagination
nor both together go to the making of genius.
Love, love, love, that is the soul of genius."
- Wolfgang Amadeus Mozart

As a perfect idea of the Creator, only you can uncover your divine purpose or your own personal genius. I can only lead you in the direction of finding your purpose in life by living mine. It is up to you to search within yourself and identify your passion. You do not have to sacrifice anything to fulfill your purpose, it has been perfectly created for you. To understand your purpose, you need to remove the barriers to knowing what motivates you. What is your passion? If you feel your purpose is eluding you, explore what you view as your limitations. Your limitations are the thoughts you have when you step on the brakes. Your heart sings to an idea, then your fear jumps in and stops you because you have self-doubt. The idea that makes your heart sing is the divine idea. The one that tells you that you can't have your dreams is your fear.

Most of my blocks revolve around self-love. Once I recognized that self-love was my issue, I immediately recognized that I needed to learn how to love myself and teach others how to love themselves. My favorite thing to do now is to be with large groups of people. I exude love. People are drawn to my light and I lavish everyone with love. The love I lavish is my love for myself. I sing at the top of my lungs, I look deeply into people's eyes when speaking with them, I hug people, and freely give out compliments. I tell people I love them, and I gain my greatest fulfillment by being love.

Once you start living your purpose, you will know that you are on the right track because you will have an inner knowing that will tell you that this is the right thing. When you are living your purpose, you will feel light and free.

Once you start living your purpose, you will still encounter the negativity of others but it will no longer affect you. People will project their own fears onto you because they are not fulfilling their own purpose and are afraid to do so because of their own beliefs and limitations. They will try to convince you that you will fail. Do not believe anyone who says you will fail. They only speak to you from their own fear. Only by living your life fully and with love and passion will you affect others and show them that they can do the same. Your claiming yourself and shining brightly has the power to lift all who would tell you that you can't. By claiming your power and fearlessly pursuing your dreams, you will show others how to claim theirs.

Make a promise to yourself that you will not allow fear to keep you from your dreams, no matter what. It's only your fear. Once you decide wholeheartedly to live your divine purpose, you will find the greatest joy you have ever had because you will know that you are completely embracing your passion and purpose. Things will start happening that you thought possible only in your imagination, and this will be your reward for fulfilling your role in creation.

The universe will recognize that you are on course, and you will feel and become more in flow with the universal energies. With every baby step, you will feel as if you are on a moving walkway. Fulfilling your purpose will seem effortless because it is what you were meant to do. You will do it with joy, and you will have the entire universe on your side guiding your steps. The universe wants you to succeed because if you succeed, we all succeed; that is how significant your role is in the universal whole.

Now that you know what you have to do, how do you get started? Listen to your inner voice. We have all been equipped with an inner guide or voice to help us make the right decisions. We know the voice of our internal truth by the messages we receive. These messages are always persistent, never judgmental, never fear based, and always love based. The messages come from within you and are the voice of your inner fire and passion. Who you are has nothing to do with other people, it has everything to do with you. Only by being completely true to you will you be true to the whole.

Whatever you are meant to accomplish will improve your relationships with yourself and the rest of humanity. Claiming your part in the universal puzzle will improve your life. Your life will change and you will have challenges but if you listen to the inner dictates of your heart and remain steadfastly true to yourself, you will find love, happiness, and richness beyond all measure. Do not let fear stop you from accomplishing your purpose; it is just an illusion your ego has created to keep you from having a fulfilling and enriching life.

For most of us, recognizing our true selves takes a lifetime of searching, discovering truths, regressing to old patterns, and then recognizing ourselves again. We will take two steps forward and one step back. This is all in the plan. You created the plan because your mind is the mind of God. Each time we take those two steps forward, we see the next level that we will eventually incorporate into our lives and believe as truth. When we take the step back, we are re-evaluating what we have already learned and landing on the foundation we have already built.

Once we recognize what it is that we must do, we must teach it through our actions so we can better learn it. Everyone I interact with is my teacher and also my student. As I share my truth, I share a piece of who I am with you, and as I interact with others, I am constantly learning, growing, and changing. We are all ever-evolving beings, constantly becoming ourselves anew. The more I teach, the more I solidify my beliefs. The more I am challenged, the more I can fine tune my beliefs to form a greater understanding of who I am constantly becoming.

When you find our truth you must teach it and live it. You are the only one who can find it, it can not be found for you. I have given you a tool to help you find the parts of yourself you reject. It is up to you to recognize, acknowledge, accept, and transform your thoughts into love and release yourself from your own bonds of limitation.

What is a life purpose? From my experience and

understanding, it is using your experience in its most positive form, which enables you to affect positive change in your life. You must heal that part of yourself that you perceive to be your personal burden. When you heal, live life steadfastly according to your truth, and by your example you will heal the world.

Because my personal burden was my relationship with my body, I know what it is like not to like my body and therefore to disown part of myself. My greatest contribution to humanity, my life purpose, is to love and accept myself completely, and through my example, to show other people how to love themselves. My relationship with my body has been my self-imposed limitation. We all have different areas in which we feel limited. The symptoms of our personal limitations are different; the cure is the same.

Stephen Hawking, one of the greatest scientific minds of our century, wrote a book titled A Brief History of Time. In it, he talks about a phenomenon that was accidentally discovered by a group of engineers testing cosmic microwave background radiation. It was theorized that in the same way in which light travels, omnidirectionally, if the big bang theory were true, the universe would look the same in every direction, viewed from the original point in space where the big bang originated. These engineers accidentally found that from Earth, in any direction that they sent out waves, the matter in the universe, when measured, looked to be the same, out to the farthest reaches of space. In other words, out to the far reaches of the universe, in every direction, space seemed to be symmetrical from the point of view of the Earth. Earth seemed to be in the center of the universe. If the big bang theory were true, and light were traveling omnidirectionally, the big bang would have originated at Earth, which was not likely.

Hawking says that space is spherical and explains it like this: Take a round balloon and draw dots all around it. As the balloon expands, from each point on the balloon, it would seem as if you were in the center, because there would be no difference from one point on the balloon to another...no differentiation...so from any point on the balloon, relative to any point of view, it would seem as if each and every dot were in the center.

The thought of the universe being spherical inspires me to believe that the theory can be scaled down to include not only celestial bodies, but also human bodies. If this theory were true that any body at any time at any point is in the center of the universe, it makes sense to me that that same theory could apply to human thought waves, which are measured as electromagnetic waves.

I am inspired to believe that every human has equal potential to affect the rest of humanity the same way any celestial body would affect the universe at large. Being a sphcrical and expanding universe, each human is in the center of the universe too. The universe as we experience it is earth. Earth is our balloon, although not expanding, yet still a sphere with various points of light or people placed around it. We all have equal capacity to have our light seen and the warmth of our being felt in equal measure.

If we are living in a way in which we are being true to our purpose, and are using our own unique talents to our best ability to serve the highest good of all, we all have equal power to create a better world to live in. Each of us houses a light of equal and beauty and potential. Whatever we choose to do will either add to the light of the universe or detract from the overall light of the universe. If we fuel the light with loving actions and thoughts of self-acceptance, if we are true to ourselves, our light will shine more brightly and will be seen from a farther distance. If we choose to hide our light, or to act out of anger and fear, our light will seem diminished and shielded from the rest of the universe, which will be seemingly darker as a direct result of our choices and actions. Act in accordance with your internal dictates. If you act with integrity and love, you are well along your path to living your truth and knowing and reason for your existence.

~ **Nothing To Fear** ~

"Never the spirit was born; the spirit shall cease never.
Never was time it was not; End and Beginning are dreams!
Birthless and deathless and changeless remaineth the spirit
forever; Death hath not touched it at all,
dead though the house it seems!" - Bhagavadgita

The verse above from the Bhagavadgita puts fear into perspective. We are all infinite and eternal. There is no death and no birth, only the illusion of both.

We are as eternal as the universe, because we are infinite. We will never die and the part of us that animates our bodies and lives will live forever. When we all wake from our dream, the world will end; not from destruction, but from transcendence. Claim your infinite power and fulfill your divine purpose. Until you claim your power, you will deny yourself the bliss that is your birthright and deny humanity the gift of your grace. Share all of everything you have with everyone. As you share and extend yourself, you shall receive the abundance of everything you extend.

Listen within and meditate on your questions. Your inner voice will guide you to the next step you need to take in order to fulfill your Divine Purpose. I have all the faith in you in the world, because I know the true you. You are a powerful, limitless, divine being who chosen to be here on Earth to bless me and everyone else with the gift of your brilliance.

I would like to close with a short sermon I wrote that was the result of a "Build Your Own Theology" course I took at a Unitarian Universalist Church:

"I believe that we are all part of the universal whole, or God. It is as if we are all parts of a giant puzzle with our own unique traits and characteristics. We all have our special place in the puzzle, and without each of us, the puzzle is incomplete. We may not even recognize that the person we see on the street is the same as us. If the puzzle was of a garden, we may see the other person as a piece of a flower and ourselves as a piece of garden pond. Every piece works together to create the magnificent Universal masterpiece.

I believe that we are all made of love and this is the aspect of humanity that I attribute to God. I feel there is only truth, which is the recognition of God, and everything else is misconception. I believe we are all creations of perfection for I do not believe that God makes anyone or anything imperfect. If we feel we are imperfect, it is only because we have wrongly believed the false judgments and perceptions of ourselves and others.

I believe that before birth, we decide what we will do in this lifetime. We decide crucial interactions between one another and form contracts with one another in order to help us to grow and remember what we are here to do. We contract with each other out of love for one another. I believe that the most hurtful experiences are those that we learn most from and therefore are the ones that are parts of our contracts.

I believe that those who we thought had hurt us the most are actually the ones who illuminate our paths to seeing our own perfection. I believe that as humans, we learn through contrast, and all the negative thoughts we have about ourselves are the exact opposite pole of the lessons we are here to learn. I believe those who hurt us the most actually give us our greatest gifts and provide the ashes from which our spirits rise.

I believe that we are led by fate. This is not to say that we do not have choices. I believe that in every circumstance, there are many choices we can make and still remain on the "right path." The destination will remain the same; however, the trip may be lengthened or shortened by the choices we make. I believe that we are all guided, and if we listen to our hearts, we will know the right decisions to make in any situation.

I believe we are first guided by hearing a faint whisper that we should do something. If we don't act on our guidance, we will have a stronger urge to do it. If we still don't act, we will be urged more and more strongly until we finally take action. If we don't take action or numb our senses through techniques such as binging, drinking, or drug use, we may find ourselves in a crisis. Crisis is when the universe forces us to do something because we have severely diverted from our chosen path.

I believe we are all here to help each other find enlightenment and true happiness. I believe that without every one of us, God is incomplete, and only through the happiness and enlightenment of the whole can even one eyelash of creation know the ultimate truth and enlightenment.

Most of all, I believe that we must take action on our chosen path once we figure out what it is. The fulfillment of our part of the puzzle is our purpose. For one of us to transcend this world, we must all help each other recognize where we fit in the universal puzzle and transcend together as one...as God."

Kerri Kannan has consciously been on the path toward self-realization for nearly fifteen years. After years of studying various spiritual paths, she found that spiritual realization is a process of releasing belief systems rather than acquiring knowledge. She found that no religion, doctrine or philosophy had the answers for her and the only way to discover her true nature was to forge her own path toward personal liberation and authenticity.

Kerri is the former president of Wholeness Center, Inc., and an active member of Unity church. She is a Toastmaster and has spoken for Unity churches, women's wellness weekends and various holistic events. Kerri's current projects include the creation of a spiritually centered internet networking community as well as a spiritually centered co-housing community.

Kerri Kannan lives in upstate New York with her two beautiful daughters and her cat, Nino.

Kerri Kannan can be contacted by visiting:

http://www.kerrikannan.com

INNERCIRCLE PUBLISHING

Catalog of Original Titles

ISBN	Title
0-9720080-9-8	the sometimes girl by Lisa Zaran
0-9720080-5-5	A Metaphysical Interpretation of the Bible by Dr. Steven Hairfield
0-9720080-2-0	Return To Innocence by Dr. Steven Hairfield
0-9720080-3-9	Interview With An American Monk by Dr. Steven Hairfield
0-9720080-4-7	Interview II: Heath and Healing by Dr. Steven Hairfield
0-9723191-4-X	Poetry to Touch the Heart and Soul by Marla Wienandt
0-9755214-9-7	Touched by Spirit by Marla Wienandt
0-9723191-8-2	Stress Fractures by Andew Lewis
0-9723191-7-4	One Hundred Keys to the Kingdom by Prince Camp, Jr.
0-9723191-0-7	the voice by Rick LaFerla
0-9755214-0-3	On the Edge of Deceny by Rick LaFerla
0-9723191-5-8	A Day in the Mind by Chad Lilly
0-9755214-6-2	uncommon sense by Chad Lilly
0-9755214-7-0	Peace Knights of the Soul by Dr. Jon Snodgrass
0-9755214-1-1	Petals of a Flower by Patricia McHenry
0-9755214-2-X	Poetry-Prose-Stories by J.L. Montgomery
0-9762924-0-8	The Weave that Binds Us by Martin Burke
0-9762924-2-4	Dare to Question by Jack Perrine
0-9762974-2-6	The Twelve Mastery Teachings of Christ by Lea Chapin
0-9762924-3-2	Alnombak by Ken Delnero
0-9762924-7-5	Life is a Song Worth Singing by Clarissa LeVonne Bolding
0-9762974-3-4	The Spirit Within by Susan Marie Ratcliffe
0-9720080-8-X	And the Angels Spoke by Rebecca J. Steiger
1-882918-00-2	From Ashes To Angel Light by Rebecca J. Steiger
0-9762974-6-9	The One Minute Miracle by Daniel Millstein
0-9762974-5-0	Unemployed: A Memoir by Reginald L.Goodwin
1-882918-03-7	Look and Remember by Marie taBonne
1-882918-02-9	Poetry of Comfort and Light by Marla Wienandt
1-882918-01-0	Life Happened Here by Marilyn Wendler
0-9728127-2-5	The Nature of the Self by Douglas H. Melloy
1-882918-04-5	Seven Stars: Mystical Poetry by Michaela Selfer
1-882918-05-3	Esoteric Dictionary by Christine A. Hale

Are You Aware?

www.innercirclepublishing.com

Printed in the United States
200667BV00006B/1-30/A